The Ultimate Guide to
GospeLink™

A Handbook for Speakers, Teachers, Students, and Families

Larry A. Scoffield

Jack M. Lyon

Deseret Book Company · Salt Lake City, Utah

Library of Congress Catalog Card Number 98-74850

ISBN 1-57345-400-1

Printed in the United States of America   71976-6384

10 9 8 7 6 5 4 3 2 1

Table of Contents

Acknowledgments

Working on GospeLink (with the help of many others) was probably the most demanding thing we've ever done. We'd like to thank all who were down in the trenches with us, especially Gary Frederickson (Folio expert and all-around computer guru) and Matt McBride (Renaissance man), who know where the books are buried.

We'd also like to thank our unsung cohorts Robin Shinkle, Lincoln Fillmore, Scott Davies, and Don Thorpe, and Deseret Book's publishing and marketing staffs, including Suzanne Brady, Richard Erickson, Bronwyn Evans, Tonya Facemyer, Linda Gundry, Eric Jamison, Dave McDonald, Patricia Parkinson, Jay Parry, Richard Peterson, Anne Sheffield, Ron Stucki, Kent Ware, and many others, with special appreciation to Emily Watts and Jennifer Adams.

In addition, we're grateful for the support, counsel, encouragement, and patience of Deseret Book's management team, especially Ron Millett, Sheri Dew, Tom Mabey, Keith Hunter, Gary Swapp, Roger Toone, and Don Gull.

In the production of this book, we'd like to thank Jennifer Adams, our skilled and genial editor; Ron Stucki, our peerless designer; and Patricia Parkinson, our painstaking typographer.

Finally, and most of all, we're grateful to our wives and families for their patient support; we promise to go camping *next* summer.

INTRODUCTION

In the heart of downtown Salt Lake City is the headquarters of Deseret Book Company. If you were to visit there, you might be able to see the Deseret Book library, a collection of thousands of publications dating from 1866, the year the company began. Among these volumes are some of the greatest works of LDS scholarship, doctrine, biography, history, and practical advice ever published, and if you had access to this library, you could study the gospel in a way that is impossible for most people.

But now you don't have to visit the Deseret Book library to have access to all these books. Now the finest works of LDS literature are available on GospeLink so you can read and study on your personal computer in ways you have never been able to before—in fact, in ways that would be impossible in a physical library.

In GospeLink, you'll find the classics of LDS literature, both early and modern. Nowhere else will you find a collection containing more of the words of the prophets of our day. GospeLink includes the words not only of Joseph Smith and Brigham Young, but of all the prophets through Howard W. Hunter and Gordon B. Hinckley. It also offers many of the most recent publications from Deseret Book. In addition, it includes an enormous collection of Church periodicals, reference works, and world classics.

The only problem with all of this is that there's so *much* information. If you figure that a typical six-by-nine-inch book has about 350 characters per page, then the GospeLink library contains more than 300,000 pages. That's quite a collection! So your first question might be, "How am I going to find the specific information I need?"

If you've used other electronic reference libraries, you know they're largely centered on being able to *search* for information—to "query" for words and phrases. GospeLink allows you to search in the same way, of course, and even includes additional customized features to make searching more simple and effective. GospeLink also includes a wide variety of other software features that make studying the gospel easier than ever before.

But what really sets GospeLink apart is the editorial content it includes to help you find what you need. That's not the text of the books themselves; it's additional information that has been added "on top" of the books—information about the information. Adding this information can't be done by a computer. It can be done only by an editor—and in the case of GospeLink, by dozens of editors. So what did these editors do?

1. They compiled the indexes of the LDS books to create the Comprehensive Index, which makes it possible to find information on literally thousands of topics without wading through "hits" from a search.

2. They categorized books and talks by topic, type of author, and other criteria. That means you can see all of the conference talks on faith, for example, with the click of a mouse. Or all of the books about Church history. Or all of the talks by members of the Twelve. This kind of information is what powers GospeLink Explorer, GospeLink's intelligent card catalog—a truly remarkable tool. The information is also used to provide dozens of built-in, predefined Search Sets.

3. They read through the LDS books to identify informative passages on a wide variety of gospel topics. These passages have been incorporated into the LDS Virtual Encyclopedia, which is a great tool in preparing a lesson or talk.

4. They went through every issue of the *Ensign* from 1971 through 1997, listing the articles by author, type of author, title, feature, topic, and so on. Then they compiled this information in the Ensign Index, which lets you identify *Ensign* articles in a variety of ways. For example, you can identify all of the conference talks by President Gordon B. Hinckley on pioneers. Or all of the "Mormon Journals" on prayer. Or every "I Have a Question" on the Book of Mormon. This powerful tool helps you find the information you need.

5. They wrote or compiled information about individual books in the library so you can read *about* a book you think might be interesting. You can also read about the book's author. This is like picking up a book in the bookstore and reading its jacket flaps.

6. They also went through the scriptures to identify important passages and group them in useful ways, such as stories, miracles, and parables. That means if you're looking for the parable of the Good Samaritan, for example, you can find it quickly and easily.

This book is organized in six parts.

Part 1, "Getting Started," helps you get GospeLink up and running and gives you a good introduction to GospeLink and the basics you'll need to know to use the program.

Part 2, "Using the Text Windows," gives you an overview of GospeLink's three main windows: the Scriptures window, the Books window, and the References window. The information in GospeLink is almost always accessed through these main windows.

Part 3, "Using the Main Toolbar," gives step-by-step instructions for using the powerful features of GospeLink. In this section you'll learn everything from searching for information to creating personal text notes to using the Ensign Index and Composer—the word processor included with GospeLink. This section includes an abundance of information on GospeLink Explorer, a powerful and important tool for navigating the GospeLink library.

Part 4, "Using PalmPilot," is a short section for those who own a PalmPilot, a "personal digital assistant" from 3Com, and want to use it with GospeLink.

In part 5, "Using the LDS Quotations Library," you'll learn how to access and use the Quotations Library included with GospeLink.

Part 6, "Getting the Most from GospeLink," includes advice, ideas, and practical tips for writing talks and lessons, preparing family home evenings, personalizing and researching your GospeLink library, and using GospeLink as it was meant to be used—to truly study the gospel of Jesus Christ.

To get the most out of GospeLink, browse through this book from beginning to end, marking the areas that look most interesting. That will give you a broad overview of what GospeLink can do. Then go back through the book and read in detail the areas you've marked, trying the features in the program itself. Before long, you'll be a GospeLink expert!

Please note that much of the material in parts two, three, and four of this book is adapted from the GospeLink Help System, which comes with GospeLink. The material is organized and arranged here as an easy-to-access reference guide; in addition, we have added tips and examples to make the information even more useful. And we think you will find the information in part 6, "Getting the Most from GospeLink," especially practical and helpful as you use GospeLink from day to day. We hope you enjoy *The Ultimate Guide to GospeLink*.

PART 1: GETTING STARTED

CHAPTER 1
SETTING UP GOSPELINK

ADJUSTING YOUR COMPUTER SETTINGS

Like other computer programs, GospeLink runs best on a fast computer with plenty of memory. The recommended minimum is a Pentium processor with 16 megabytes of RAM. If you're considering upgrading your computer, increased RAM will make the most difference in the speed at which GospeLink runs. The speed of your CD-ROM drive is also important—the faster, the better. In fact, the second most important upgrade you could make for running GospeLink would be to a faster CD-ROM drive. Drives with a speed of 32X are now common, although even a 4X drive will work.

If your monitor is set to a low resolution like 640 x 480, you won't be able to see as much text at one time in GospeLink's windows as you might like. If GospeLink Explorer is open at this low resolution, it will cover most of the screen. To use GospeLink most effectively, you should set your screen resolution to 800 x 600 or even higher. In addition, GospeLink will display better on your screen if you use the 16-bit color setting, referred to in Windows display settings as "High Color." Even better is 24-bit color or higher (called "True Color").

 TO ADJUST YOUR SCREEN COLOR SETTINGS AND RESOLUTION:

1. Click the **Start** button on the status bar at the bottom of your screen.
2. Click **Settings.**
3. Click **Control Panel.**
4. Double-click the **Display** icon.

5. Click the **Settings** tab.

6. Set Colors on the left of the window. Select "High Color (16-bit)" or higher.

7. Set Screen Area (resolution) on the right of the window. Select 800 x 600 or higher.

8. When you're finished, click **OK** to save your settings.

9. Follow any additional instructions that appear on your screen.

INSTALLING GOSPELINK ON YOUR COMPUTER

 AUTOMATIC INSTALLATION:

To install GospeLink on your computer automatically, follow these steps:

1. Begin at the Windows desktop.

2. Carefully insert the Installation Disk into your CD-ROM drive with the printed side up.

3. Wait for the installation instructions to appear on your screen.

4. Follow the instructions to install GospeLink on your computer.

 MANUAL INSTALLATION:

If for some reason the automatic installation does not work, follow these steps:

1. Begin at the Windows desktop.

2. Carefully insert the Installation Disk into your CD-ROM drive with the printed side up.

3. Click the **Start** button on the taskbar and choose **Run.**

4. Type **d:\setup.exe** in the line labeled **Open.** (If your CD-ROM drive uses a letter other than **d**, substitute that letter for **d**.)

5. Click the **OK** button and follow the on-screen instructions to install GospeLink.

STARTING THE PROGRAM

 TO START THE GOSPELINK PROGRAM:

1. Put GospeLink Disk A or B into your computer's CD-ROM drive.

2. Click the **Start** button on the Windows taskbar.

3. Click the **Programs** folder.

4. Click the **GospeLink** folder.

5. Click the **GospeLink** icon.

The start-up animation will be displayed, and the GospeLink program will start. As it starts, it will load several libraries and special features. This may take a few moments.

NOTE: You can skip the start-up animation in the future by clicking the **Options** button on the main toolbar and clicking **Skip Start-up Animation.**

VERIFYING YOUR SERIAL NUMBER AND USER NAME

The first time you start GospeLink, you'll see this "Welcome to GospeLink" message, which will allow you to verify your serial number and user name.

Please check the serial number to make sure it matches the number on the back of your CD case. You'll need this number to obtain technical support for GospeLink. While using GospeLink, you can find this number by clicking the **Help** button on the main toolbar and then clicking **About.** The number will be displayed in the About window.

When you installed GospeLink, you entered your name. You can use that name as your user name for signing on to GospeLink, or you can change the user name here.

Click **OK** to make your changes permanent and start the GospeLink program.

SIGNING ON

If this is the first time you've used GospeLink, and you've just created your first user name, you're already "signed on" to GospeLink. This is also true if your user name is the only one you've created.

If you've added other user names, however, you may need to sign on to GospeLink by selecting your user name from the list of user names. You do this on the start-up screen next to the question "Who Are You?"

 TO SELECT A USER:

1. Click the down arrow in the **Who Are You?** box to see the list of user names.

2. Sign on by clicking the name of your choice.

NOTE: GospeLink remembers its last user and will display that user as the default when it is started. If you were the last one to use GospeLink, your user name will already be displayed, which means that you are already signed on.

After you've signed on, you can press the **Enter** key to jump directly to the main screen, or you can select one of the other options on the start-up screen.

THE START-UP SCREEN

GospeLink's start-up screen looks like this:

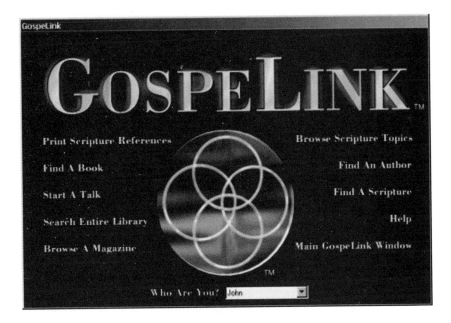

The screen has a list of things you can do when starting GospeLink:

Print Scripture References	Starts GospeLink with Scripture Guide and PrePrint opened. Lets you find scriptures and then copy them to PrePrint to be printed.
Find A Book	Starts GospeLink with Book Guide opened. Lets you find a specific book in the library and go to it.
Start A Talk	Starts GospeLink with Composer opened. Lets you begin a talk or lesson. (If you plan to use your own word processor, you may not need this option.)

Search Entire Library	Starts GospeLink with the Search window opened. Lets you search the entire library or limit the search to specific items.
Browse A Magazine	Starts GospeLink with GospeLink Explorer opened to the Periodicals tab. Lets you browse GospeLink's periodicals.
Browse Scripture Topics	Starts GospeLink with GospeLink Explorer opened to the Topics tab. Lets you find scriptures on a selected topic.
Find An Author	Starts GospeLink with GospeLink Explorer opened to the Authors tab. Lets you search for an author and view all of that author's works.
Find A Scripture	Starts GospeLink with Scripture Guide opened. Lets you find a specific scripture reference and go to it.
Help	Starts GospeLink's help system.
Main GospeLink Window	Starts GospeLink's main window. This is the default; if you simply press your Enter key, this is the action that will be taken.

You can choose any of these options, but if this is the first time you've used GospeLink, try choosing **Main GospeLink Window.** You can do this by hitting your **Enter** key or by clicking **Main GospeLink Window** with the mouse. When you do, GospeLink's main window will open.

Once you are in the main window, you will want to navigate GospeLink through the main toolbar at the top of the screen rather than returning to the start-up screen. If you need to return to the start-up screen, however, you can do this by clicking the **Tools** button on the main toolbar and selecting **Switch to a Different User** from the drop-down menu.

NOTE: You can skip the start-up screen in the future by clicking the **Options** button on the main toolbar and clicking **Skip Start-up Screen.** If you do this, GospeLink will start with the default user name, and other users will be unable to sign on. This option is provided for situations where only one person will be using GospeLink.

ADDING USERS

You can create user names for other members of your family. This allows each user to have his or her own highlighting, bookmarks, personal notes, and so on.

 TO CREATE A NEW USER:

1. Start the GospeLink program.
2. Click the down arrow next to the question "Who Are You?"
3. Click **Add a New User.**

4. The following window will appear:

5. Enter the new user's name in the text box and click the **Add** button. The new user will be added and the window will disappear.

TIP:	You can create a user name for each of your study or research projects. For example, if you were interested in researching the geography of the Book of Mormon, you could create a user name called "Book of Mormon Geography" and sign on with that name every time you did that kind of research. You can have as many as 500 user names.

DELETING USERS

You can delete user names you have already created.

 TO DELETE A USER:

1. Start the GospeLink program.
2. Click the down arrow next to the question "Who Are You?"
3. Click **Add a New User.**

Who Are You? | Add a New User... | ▼

4. The following window will appear:

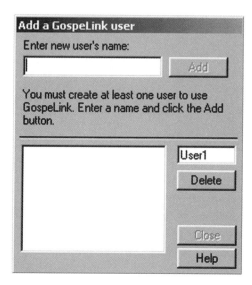

Add a GospeLink user

Enter new user's name:

[   ] | Add |

You must create at least one user to use GospeLink. Enter a name and click the Add button.

| User1 |
| Delete |

| Close |
| Help |

5. Select the user to be deleted and then click the **Delete** button. The user will be completely removed from GospeLink.

WARNING! If you delete a user, that user's highlighting, bookmarks, personal notes, and other personalized items will be removed. Be careful not to delete the wrong user name.

WHAT'S ON THE COMPACT DISKS

The GospeLink library is so large that it fills several compact disks. These disks are organized in a logical way so you can find the information you need. You can switch the disks anytime while using GospeLink.

Installation Disk	Contains the GospeLink setup program, which installs GospeLink on your computer. This disk also contains the Tutorial (to help you learn to use GospeLink) and the LDS Quotations Library (available after you register).
Disk A	Contains works by General Authorities and other LDS authors.
Disk B	Contains Church periodicals (including *Journal of Discourses* and Conference Reports) and the World Classics Library.

GospeLink installs certain works on your computer's hard drive. These works are available even if you're not using Disk A or Disk B. They include

- The standard works (Old Testament, New Testament, Book of Mormon, Doctrine and Covenants, and Pearl of Great Price).
- The Joseph Smith Translation of the Bible.
- The complete Comprehensive Index (optional—if you prefer, you can use the abridged version while using Disk A).
- Folio Views 4.1 (optional—for previous users of Folio Views who prefer that interface).

NOTE: The Apocrypha, Pseudepigrapha, and Early Christian Writings are included on Disk B as part of the World Classics Library. You can access the Old Testament Apocrypha, Old Testament Pseudepigrapha, and New Testament Pseudepigrapha under those names in the Books tab of GospeLink Explorer (see pages 118–24) and in the table of contents in the Non-LDS Authors view under "Various Authors." You can also find the early Christian writings under their individual titles as listed in appendix 2.

SWITCHING DISKS

 TO SWITCH THE COMPACT DISKS:

    1. Click the **Tools** button on the toolbar at the top of the main window. A menu will appear.

    2. Click **Switch Disks.** The following message box will appear, prompting you to switch the disks:

    3. Open your CD-ROM drive and switch the disks. When the light on your CD-ROM drive stops flashing, click the **OK** button. GospeLink will display the information from the new disk.

NOTE: If you switch disks without using this procedure, GospeLink will automatically detect the new disk and display the message box above. Click **OK** to complete the switch. Scripture Guide, Book Guide, Search, and GospeLink Explorer will close to allow for the switch in disks.

TIP: If your computer has two CD-ROM drives, you can use both disks at the same time. Put Disk A in one drive and Disk B in the other. If you have only one drive, you might want to consider installing a second one. Or, if you have a large hard drive with plenty of room to spare (at least 1.2 gigabytes), you may want to install the entire library on it. This will greatly increase the speed at which GospeLink runs and make it possible to use all of the libraries at the same time. For information on how to do this, visit the GospeLink Web site at www.gospelink.com or contact GospeLink technical support.

FOLIO VIEWS USERS

If you are an experienced Folio user, you can use the Folio Views 4.1 interface with the GospeLink library.

 TO START FOLIO VIEWS 4.1:

1. Click the **Start** button on the Windows taskbar.
2. Click the **Programs** folder.
3. Click the **GospeLink** folder.
4. Click the **Folio** folder.
5. Click the **Folio Views 4.1** icon.

WARNING! Many features of GospeLink are not available in the Folio Views 4.1 interface, and the GospeLink documentation does not cover its use. It is included for previous Folio Views users who prefer that interface.

CHAPTER 2

GOSPELINK BASICS

GospeLink closely follows the Windows standard for menus, toolbars, list boxes, mouse use, and scroll bars. If you understand how to run a Windows application, you'll be able to operate GospeLink quickly and easily. If you need more information about how to run Windows applications, see the standard Windows Help system. To do so:

1. Click the **Start** button on the Windows taskbar.
2. Click the **Help** icon.
3. Click the item you are interested in learning about.

USING SCROLL BARS

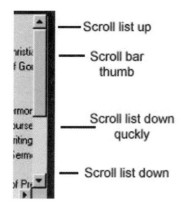

The GospeLink scroll bars work like standard Windows scroll bars:

- Click on the top arrow to scroll the list up.
- Click on the bottom arrow to scroll the list down.
- Click and hold the mouse button on the bar between the arrows, the "scroll bar thumb," to scroll the list up or down by dragging the bar in the direction you wish to scroll.
- Click on the space between one of the arrows and the scroll bar thumb to scroll up or down one screen at a time.

NOTE: In all of the GospeLink list boxes, if you use the scroll bar thumb to scroll the list, a small window will appear and display the items on the list as you scroll by them. This will help you know where you are on the list.

USING THE MOUSE

The mouse is very important in using GospeLink. You'll use it to select items and navigate through the library.

LEFT MOUSE BUTTON

Most of the time, you'll use the left mouse button to push buttons, select tabs, select hypertext words, use drop-down lists, select items in a list, change window sizes, and so on.

NOTE: Whenever these instructions ask you to "click" something, that usually means you should point at the object with the mouse pointer and then quickly press and release the left mouse button. To "double-click" is to click twice in quick succession. If you're not yet comfortable using the mouse, you will be after a little practice.

RIGHT MOUSE BUTTON

Clicking the right mouse button activates pop-up menus wherever they are available.

MOUSE POINTER

The mouse pointer appears differently depending on which part of GospeLink the pointer is over. If the pointer is over a button, for example, it will change to a pointing hand. Here are the different forms the pointer can take:

☝	This pointing hand indicates that whatever the hand is over can be clicked. The hand may be over a button, a list, linked text, or a tab. If you click the mouse button when this cursor is displayed, something will happen.
↖	This single arrow is the normal mouse pointer.

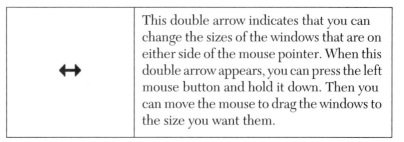	This double arrow indicates that you can change the sizes of the windows that are on either side of the mouse pointer. When this double arrow appears, you can press the left mouse button and hold it down. Then you can move the mouse to drag the windows to the size you want them.

DRAGGING

Dragging is moving something with the mouse pointer. A good example is the use of the scroll bars found in GospeLink. As discussed earlier, each scroll bar has a "scroll bar thumb," the bar or slider between the two arrows of the scroll bar. To use the scroll bar thumb:

1. Point the mouse at the thumb.
2. Press and hold down the left mouse button.
3. Move the mouse up or down to scroll through the list.

Another example of dragging is changing the sizes of the windows on the main GospeLink screen. To change the size of the Scriptures window:

1. Move the mouse pointer between the Scriptures window and the Books window. The pointer should turn into a double arrow, like this:

2. Press and hold down the left mouse button.
3. Move the mouse to the right to increase the size of the Scriptures window. Move it to the left to make the window smaller.
4. Release the mouse button.

SELECTING TEXT

There are several ways to select text for copying, highlighting, and so on.

 TO SELECT TEXT BY DRAGGING THE MOUSE:

1. Move the mouse pointer to the beginning of the text.
2. Press and hold down the left mouse button.

3. Drag the mouse to select the text. The text will be highlighted in a different color.

4. Release the mouse button.

The text will be selected.

 TO SELECT TEXT BY CLICKING WITH THE MOUSE:

1. Move the mouse pointer to the beginning of the text.

2. Insert the cursor by clicking with the left mouse button.

3. Hold down the **Shift** key.

4. Move the mouse pointer to the ending of the text.

5. Click with the left mouse button.

The text will be selected and highlighted in a different color.

 TO SELECT TEXT FOR DROP-DOWN AND POP-UP MENUS:

Click anywhere in a paragraph.

The paragraph will not be highlighted, but it will be selected.

UNDERSTANDING "FOCUS"

When you're working on a GospeLink screen, the part you are working on is the part that has the focus. If you click on an item in a list, the list will have the focus. If you click on a text box where you will type information, the text box will have the focus. Another way of describing focus is to say that a window or list is "active."

Focus is important to understand so you can operate the many list boxes in GospeLink. If you click on a list box, it will have the focus, and all your keystrokes will be applied to that list.

When a list box has the focus:

• The selected item is highlighted in a different color.

• You can press a letter key to jump to that section of the alphabet within a list box. For example, if you press **F**, the list will jump to the first item that begins with the letter F.

• You can scroll the list with the arrow keys and the **Page Up** and **Page Down** keys.

On the main GospeLink screen, only one of the three text windows (Scriptures, Books, or References) can have the focus at one time. The window that has the focus will react to all of your keystrokes, such as **Page Up** and **Page Down.** To move the focus to one of the windows, click in that window with the mouse. For example, if you wanted to move through the Books window with the **Page Down** key, you would point at the window with the mouse and click the left mouse button. Then you would use the **Page Down** key to scroll through the text.

DISPLAY LABELS

Often when you click on a title or some other item in a list or window, you'll see the name of the item in a display label. Here's what a typical display label looks like:

Gen. 1:8

A display label tells you which item in a list or window is currently selected. If you're not sure what is currently selected, look in the display label associated with that list or window.

USING DROP-DOWN LISTS

Drop-down lists let you choose an item from a list of items. You'll find drop-down lists throughout GospeLink. The drop-down list in the picture below is from the Scripture Explorer window. It lets you choose a Scripture Set.

Scripture Sets
Miracles: New Testament

You can identify a drop-down list by the down arrow on the right of the list. The down arrow looks like this:

There are two ways to activate a drop-down list:
- Click the down arrow with the mouse.
- Click the text box with the mouse.

The list will appear:

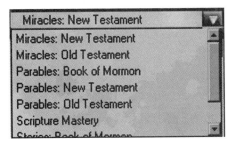

To find an item in the list, use the scroll bar on the right of the list.

To choose an item, click it with the mouse. The item you clicked will be highlighted as the chosen item.

SELECTING FROM A LIST

GospeLink has many lists that categorize items to help you find what you're looking for, such as lists of books, authors, types of books, Search Sets, Scripture Sets, and so on. Here's an example of a typical list:

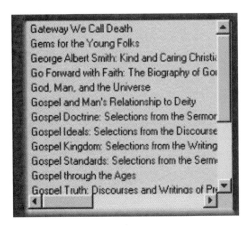

 TO SELECT AN ITEM FROM A LIST:

Click the item you want to select. The selected item will be highlighted in a different color. You can move the highlighting up or down to different items with the arrow keys on your keyboard. You can also press the **Page Up** and **Page Down** keys to move through the list more quickly.

After selecting an item (which sets the focus on the list), you can press a letter key to jump to the first item in the list that begins with that letter. For example, in a complete list of books, pressing **S** would jump to *Sacred Truths of the Doctrine and Covenants, vol. 1,* the first book to begin with S in the list. If you pressed **S** again, the next item that starts with S would be selected.

The scroll bar can be used to scroll the list up and down. When you drag the scroll bar thumb up or down, a small window opens showing the current item. This lets you see where you are as you scroll.

 WAYS TO SCROLL A LIST:

- Select an item, then press the arrow keys to move up and down the list.
- Select an item and press the **Page Up** or **Page Down** keys to move the list a section at a time.
- Click on the scroll bar arrows.
- Click on the area above or below the scroll bar thumb.
- Click on the scroll bar thumb and drag it up or down.

NOTE: If you want to read an item whose title is longer than the box is wide, point the mouse at the item and let the pointer rest for a second or two. A box containing the full title will appear.

USING OUTLINE LISTS

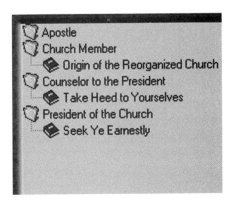

Outline lists are similar to other lists in GospeLink and work in much the same way. However, outline lists contain information that can be grouped into folders. Each folder is represented by an icon (a small picture) like this:

at the left of its name. Folders are not items as books, talks, and poems are; folders are containers for other items. When you click on a folder, the items it contains are displayed below it. Click the folder again, and the items disappear back into the folder. Folders can contain other folders.

Like folders, items in an outline list are also indicated by icons, such as these:

Items don't contain other items as folders do. An item can be selected like anything else on a list.

Here are the outline list icons and what they represent:

	Folder that contains other folders or items
	Book
	Talk, poem, or story

 TO SELECT AN ITEM FROM AN OUTLINE LIST:

Click the item you want to select. The selected item will be highlighted in a different color. You can move the highlighting up or down to different items with the arrow keys on your keyboard. You can also press the **Page Up** and **Page Down** keys to move through the list more quickly.

After selecting an item (which sets the focus on the list), you can press a letter key to jump to the first item in the list that begins with that letter. For example, in a complete list of books, pressing **B** would jump to *Be of Good Cheer*, the first book to begin with B in the list. If you pressed **B** again, the next item that starts with B would be selected.

The scroll bar can be used to scroll the list up and down. When you drag the scroll bar thumb up or down, a small window opens showing the current item. This lets you see where you are as you scroll.

 WAYS TO SCROLL AN OUTLINE LIST:

- Select an item, then press the arrow keys to move up and down the list.
- Select an item and press the **Page Up** or **Page Down** keys to move the list a page at a time.
- Click on the scroll bar arrows.
- Click on the area above or below the scroll bar thumb.
- Click on the scroll bar thumb and drag it up or down.

NOTE: If you want to read an item whose title is longer than the box is wide, point the mouse at the item and let the pointer rest for a second or two. A box containing the full title will appear.

USING TOOLBARS

Toolbars are commonly used in Windows applications to start various parts of a program or to perform certain functions within a program. Toolbars consist of buttons you can click. The buttons have icons to help you remember what they do. The buttons also have Tooltips, which are small message boxes that appear if the mouse pointer remains over the button for a second or two. Tooltips briefly describe what the buttons do.

 TO USE A TOOLBAR:

1. Identify which button will perform the function you want. (If you're not sure which button to use, try reading the Tooltips.)
2. Click the button with the mouse.

SAMPLE GOSPELINK TOOLBARS

The following toolbar appears on GospeLink's main screen. Its buttons include some text to help you know what they do.

This next toolbar is the PrePrint toolbar. Its buttons have no explanatory text, but their Tooltips will remind you what the buttons do.

USING TOOLTIPS

Tooltips give you more information about buttons, tabs, and other items. For example, if you're not sure what a button on a toolbar does, move the mouse pointer to the button and let it rest for a second or two. A small box will appear with a brief description of the button's function. If you move the mouse, the tip will disappear. Here's what a Tooltip looks like:

The Tooltip in the picture above is displayed by pointing the mouse at the Author tab in GospeLink Explorer. It explains that the tab will help you explore the GospeLink library by author.

Using Menus

GospeLink contains several standard Windows menus, such as those in PrePrint and Composer. Menus help you perform various functions, such as print, copy, delete, close, and so on. You can use menus with the mouse or with your keyboard. Here's the menu from Composer:

This menu has seven items to choose from: File, Edit, View, Insert, Format, Table, and Help. To open one of the menus, click it with the mouse. You can also hold down the **ALT** key and press the letter key that is underlined in the menu item. For example, you could open the File menu by holding down the **ALT** key and pressing **F.** You would then see other menu items you could choose. Here's what you'd see if you opened the File menu in Composer:

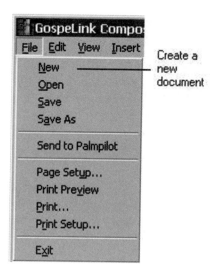

To select an item on the menu, click it with the mouse. For example, to create a new document, you'd click on the word **New.** You could also hold down the **ALT** key and press **N.**

SHORTCUT KEYS

Standard Windows shortcut keys are used for some menu items. For example, holding down **CTRL** and pressing **C** will copy selected text to the Windows Clipboard. This shortcut key works in Composer as well as the text windows. Another shortcut key you'll probably use a lot is holding down **CTRL** and pressing **V**, which pastes text from the Windows Clipboard into another application, such as your word processor.

USING POP-UP MENUS

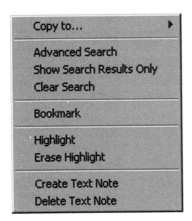

GospeLink has many areas where you can use pop-up menus. To use a pop-up menu, point the mouse at a list, some text, or another item. Then click the *right* mouse button. A small menu will appear with a list of things you can do with the item you clicked. On the GospeLink main screen, you can click the text windows with the right mouse button to do all kinds of things, including copying, printing, searching, and so on.

Pop-up menus operate much like regular menus, except they appear where you need them. To select a menu item in a pop-up menu, click it with the *left* mouse button.

USING HYPERTEXT

Hypertext is text that is linked to other text. (In a printed book, you'd call it a cross-reference.) For example, in the quotation below, the scripture references would appear in blue on your screen.

> Peter, in tribute to the Master, noted how Jesus was reviled but "when he was reviled, reviled not again." (1 Peter 2:23.) Alma's counsel to us is: "Do not revile against those who do cast you out." (Alma 34:40.) We are told even to avoid reviling against revilers. (D&C 19:30.) And again, "revile not against those that revile." (D&C 31:9.)

These blue references are examples of hypertext. (Hypertext may also appear in other colors.) If you clicked on one of the hypertext scripture references, you'd jump to that scripture in the Scriptures window. The GospeLink library contains thousands of hypertext links that will help make your gospel study more effective.

 TO USE HYPERTEXT:

    1. Point at the hypertext with the mouse. The pointer will change to a pointing hand.

    2. Press the left mouse button to jump to the linked text.

USING THE WINDOWS CLIPBOARD

The Windows Clipboard is a place in your computer's memory where you can temporarily store copied information. Then you can paste that information into different applications. For example, you might use GospeLink to find a quotation for a lesson or a talk. Then you could select the quotation, copy it into the Windows Clipboard, and paste it from the Clipboard into your word processor.

 TO USE THE WINDOWS CLIPBOARD:

    1. Select the text you want to copy.

    2. Hold down the **CTRL** key on your keyboard.

    3. Press the **C** key on your keyboard.

    The selected text will be copied to the Windows Clipboard.

NOTE: You can't see what's in the Windows Clipboard. It holds only one selection at a time. Anytime you copy something to the Clipboard, it replaces what is already there.

PART 2: USING THE TEXT WINDOWS

CHAPTER 3

TEXT WINDOWS OVERVIEW

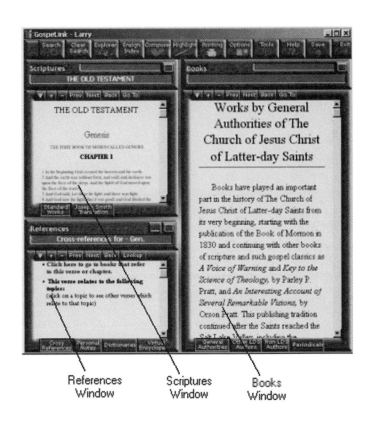

References   Scriptures   Books
Window   Window   Window

GospeLink's main screen is divided into three text windows: Scriptures window, Books window, and References window.

Each window can be resized or displayed full screen so you can see the information the way you want. Above the windows are various buttons that let you use certain features, such as changing text size, going back, and so on. Below the windows are buttons that let you see different kinds of works in each window:

Window	Works Displayed
Scriptures window	• The standard works –Old Testament –New Testament –Book of Mormon –Doctrine and Covenants –Pearl of Great Price • The complete Joseph Smith Translation of the Bible
Books window	• Works by General Authorities • Works by other LDS authors • Works by Non-LDS authors • Church periodicals **NOTE:** This window also displays the scriptures during a side-by-side comparison.
References window	• Cross-References (Topical Guide to the Scriptures [1977]) • Personal Notes • Dictionaries, including –*Dictionary of the Book of Mormon* –Webster's 1828 *American Dictionary of the English Language* –*Easton's Bible Dictionary* –*Smith's Bible Dictionary* –*Strong's Hebrew Dictionary* –*Strong's Greek Dictionary* –*LDS Virtual Encyclopedia*

SIZING THE TEXT WINDOWS

Vertical sizing bar

Horizontal sizing bar

As with other Windows applications, you can change the size of the GospeLink application window. You can also change the size of the text windows on GospeLink's main screen. This provides some real advantages in the way you work. For example, if you're interested in focusing on the scriptures while still seeing the other two windows, you can make the Scriptures window bigger than the other two windows—horizontally, vertically, or both. Also, if you want to change your screen resolution, you won't have to reload GospeLink to make it look right on your screen, as you do with some applications. (The recommended screen resolution for GospeLink is 800 x 600 or above.) If you use a high-resolution setting for your monitor and want to see your word processor and GospeLink at the same time, you can adjust the application windows to do so.

TO RESIZE THE GOSPELINK APPLICATION WINDOW:

1. Click the **Restore** button (the middle button in the top right corner of the GospeLink window) to make sure the window is not maximized.

2. Rest the mouse pointer on the edge of the window until it becomes a double arrow, like this:

3. Click and hold down the left mouse button.

4. Drag the window to the size you want.
5. Release the mouse button.

 TO RESIZE THE TEXT WINDOWS ON GOSPELINK'S MAIN SCREEN:

1. Rest the mouse pointer on the gold band between any two text windows until it becomes a double arrow, like this:

2. Click and hold down the left mouse button.
3. Drag the windows to the size you want.
4. Release the mouse button.

NOTE: The GospeLink text windows have a minimum size. You cannot make the windows any smaller than this minimum.

CHANGING DISPLAYS

You can change the way GospeLink's three text windows are displayed by clicking the display buttons, which are located in the top right corner of each window:

Display Button

There are three kinds of display buttons:

	The full-screen button displays a window full screen. For example, if you click this button on the Books window, the Books window will fill the entire GospeLink screen, hiding the Scriptures window and the References window.

	The three-window button displays all three text windows at the same time. You'll see this button on the top right corner of a window displayed full screen.
	The minimize button is found only on the References window. It minimizes the References window so you can see the Scriptures window and the Books window together for side-by-side comparisons.

When you first start GospeLink, all three text windows are displayed. You can change the size of the windows to meet your needs. The default, three-window display looks like this:

By clicking the full-screen display button on one of the three windows, you can display that window full screen. This lets you see more text at one time. It also reveals two additional tools, the Reference Area and the table of contents, which you will learn more about later. Any of the GospeLink windows can be displayed full screen. A full-screen display of the Books window looks like this:

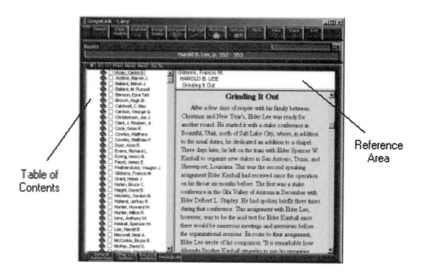

Reference
Area

Table of
Contents

By clicking the minimize button on the References window, you can
display the Scriptures window and the Books window side by side.
This lets you compare text in the two windows for truly effective
gospel study. You can compare the scriptures to other books in the
library, or to themselves. The side-by-side view looks like this:

Scriptures
Window

Books
Window

DROP-DOWN MENU

Each GospeLink text window includes a drop-down menu that lets you perform different functions with the text in the window. To see the menu, click the down arrow on the top left corner of a window. The arrow looks like this:

When you click the arrow, you'll see the following menu:

The items on the menu do the following:

Copy To	Copies selected text to one of four different areas:
	Windows Clipboard. Lets you paste the copied text into other Windows applications, such as your word processor.
	Composer. Puts the copied text directly into Composer, GospeLink's built-in word processor.
	PrePrint. Puts the copied text into PrePrint, where you can arrange copied items and print them.
	PalmPilot. Puts the copied text into a file that can be loaded directly into a PalmPilot. (You'll need this option only if you own a PalmPilot, a "personal digital assistant" from 3Com.)

Print	Copies selected text directly to PrePrint, where you can arrange copied items and print them.
Bookmark	Lets you place a bookmark in the selected text.
Highlight	Highlights selected text with the current highlighter.
Erase Highlight	Removes highlighting from the selected text.
Save	Saves highlighting, bookmarks, and so on in the current text window.

CHANGING TEXT SIZE

A A A A A **A**

GospeLink lets you change the size of the text in each window. This is useful for a number of reasons. For example, if you need to select and copy a lot of text, you might want to reduce the size so you can see large blocks of text at one time. If your eyesight isn't as good as it used to be, you might want to enlarge the text for easier reading. Or, you might want to reduce the text in windows you use less frequently and enlarge it in windows you use more frequently.

Changing text size works especially well if your monitor is set at a higher resolution, such as 1024 x 768. At a higher resolution, you can display more text in a larger area at a fairly large size.

To change the text size, click the + button or the – button at the top of a window. Each time you click the button, it enlarges or reduces the text an additional size until it has reached the end of its range.

+	Enlarges the size of the text.
–	Reduces the size of the text.

Previous and Next Buttons

Each time you search the GospeLink library, the items that match your search ("hits") will be highlighted in a text window. To move from one matched item to another, click the **Prev** and **Next** buttons.

	Moves to the previous matched item, or "hit."
Next	Moves to the next matched item, or "hit."

Back Button

The **Back** button also appears at the top of each text window. It displays the previous search performed or hypertext link made. If you search for the word *faith,* for example, and then search for the word *hope,* you can still see the results of your search for *faith* by pressing the **Back** button. You can continue to press the button to see each of your previous searches.

Go To Button

Go To

The **Go To** button lets you quickly go to a particular place within a text window. If you are in the Scriptures window, the **Go To** button takes you to a specific scripture verse. If you are in the Books window, the **Go To** button takes you to a specific page within a book. The **Go To** button works by activating the Scripture Guide or Book Guide, depending on which window you are in. (For more information, see the section on the Scripture Guide, pages 59–60 and the section on the Book Guide, pages 63–64.)

Window	Action
Scriptures window	Display the Scripture Guide.
Books window	Display the Book Guide.

NOTE: Use the Scripture Guide to start side-by-side comparison of the scriptures, which displays the scriptures in the Scriptures window and the Books window at the same time.

POP-UP MENU

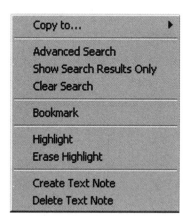

A pop-up menu, like the one above, is associated with each text window on GospeLink's main screen. This menu lets you use various features in the window to which it is attached. You can activate the pop-up menu by pointing at the window and clicking the right mouse button.

The pop-up menu includes the following options:

Copy to . . .	Copies selected text to one of four different areas:
	Windows Clipboard. Lets you paste the copied text into other Windows applications, such as your word processor.
	Composer. Puts the copied text directly into Composer, GospeLink's built-in word processor.
	PrePrint. Puts the copied text into PrePrint, where you can arrange copied items and print them.
	PalmPilot. Puts the copied text into a file that can be loaded directly into a PalmPilot. (You'll need this option only if you own a PalmPilot, a "personal digital assistant" from 3Com.)
Advanced Search	Opens the standard Folio Advanced Query dialog. Users of previous Deseret Book or Infobases software libraries will recognize this search tool. You can use Folio search syntax with this tool.
Show Search Results Only	Shows only those paragraphs containing matching items from a search. This is a toggle that you can turn on and off.
Clear Search	Removes the marking on found items and restores the text window to its original condition.
Bookmark	Lets you place a bookmark in the text.
Highlight	Highlights selected text with the current highlighter.
Erase Highlight	Removes highlighting from the selected text.

Create Text Note	Lets you place a note in the text.
Delete Text Note	Lets you delete a note in the text.

TEXT AREA

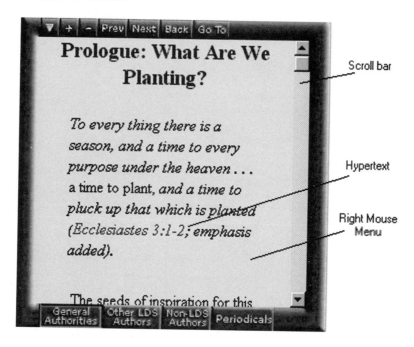

The text area is the part of a text window where information from the library is displayed. The text area includes certain features you should be aware of:

Scroll bars	The scroll bar on the right of the text area functions like a standard Windows scroll bar. Because GospeLink contains so much information, moving the scroll bar very much may take you to an entirely different book. If you want to move just a little, use the Page Up and Page Down keys.

Hypertext	Words marked in blue are hypertext links. If you click on one of these words, GospeLink will take you to the linked text. Many of these links will take you to a verse of scripture, which will be displayed in the Scriptures window.
Pop-up Menu	To see the pop-up menu, click the right mouse button in the text. You can then use one of the features on the menu.

REFERENCE AREA

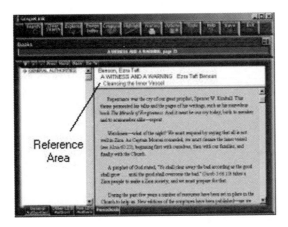

The reference area is part of a text window. When a window is displayed full screen, the reference area will appear on the top right of the text.

 TO SEE THE REFERENCE AREA:

Click a window's full-screen display button:

NOTE: You can adjust the size of the reference area by dragging the bar that separates it from the text being displayed.

The reference area shows the available information about the work being displayed. The information may include the following:

- Type of work (General Authority, LDS author, and so on)
- Author's name
- Title of the work
- Chapter headings and subheadings

PERSONAL TEXT NOTES

Use personal text notes to make notes in the library text. This is something like writing comments in the margins of a book, only you can write several paragraphs rather than just a few words. A text note stays attached to the paragraph in the library where you make it, unlike personal notes in the References window.

 TO CREATE A PERSONAL TEXT NOTE:

1. Click the paragraph where you want to create a note. If you don't do this, GospeLink won't know where to put the note you're trying to create.

2. Click the paragraph again with the right mouse button. The pop-up menu will appear.

3. Click **Create Text Note** on the pop-up menu with the left mouse button. The text note window will appear.

4. Type your note into the text note window.

5. When you're finished typing your note, click the close button (marked with an **X**) in the upper right corner of the text note window.

The location of the note will be marked with a text note icon in the library text at the beginning of the marked paragraph. The icon looks like this:

TIP: Keep notes to preserve your thoughts, feelings, and decisions as you study the scriptures and other books.

 TO EDIT A PERSONAL TEXT NOTE:

1. Go to a paragraph containing a text note icon.

2. Click the text note icon. The text note window will open.

3. Add or delete text as needed.

4. When you're finished editing your note, click the close button (marked with an **X**) in the upper right corner of the text note window.

TO DELETE A PERSONAL TEXT NOTE:

1. Go to a paragraph containing a text note icon.

2. Click the paragraph containing the note. If you don't do this, GospeLink won't know which note you're trying to delete.

3. Click the paragraph again with the right mouse button. The pop-up menu will appear.

4. Click **Delete Text Note** on the pop-up menu.

5. Confirm the deletion.

NOTE: Your text notes will be saved when you click the Save button on the main toolbar.

FOOTNOTES

In many of the books in the GospeLink library, you'll see the symbol "fn" in blue hypertext. This symbol designates a footnote.

- If you click the footnote, you'll be taken to that note at the end of the chapter where it appears.
- To get back to the text where you were, click the **Back** button at the top of the text window.

NOTE: Some footnotes appear in pop-up notes rather than at the ends of chapters. To close a pop-up note, click the close button (marked with an **X**) in the upper right corner of the pop-up window.

SEARCH RESULTS AREA

The search results area is displayed at the bottom of the text area after a search of the entire library is performed. (A search of the entire library is done by clicking the **Search** button on the main toolbar.) The search results area lists the matched items in order of their relevance. That means the most meaningful items are presented first and the least meaningful last, based on the words in your search. The ranking is determined by various criteria built into the Folio search engine.

NOTE: You can adjust the size of the search results area by dragging the bar that separates it from the main text area.

Search results are much more than just a list of matches. You can use the search results to go to the text they refer to.

TO GO TO THE TEXT LISTED IN THE SEARCH RESULTS AREA:

Double-click the item you want to see. The text for that item will appear above the search results area in the main text area. For example, in the window pictured above, you could double-click "this man of God" to go to that text in the book *Sermons and Missionary Services.*

SEARCH RESULTS POP-UP MENU

If you click with the right mouse button in the search results area, a pop-up menu will appear giving you three options:

Option	Function
Words around Hits	Displays the text around the matching words, or displays references only.
Save Column Layout	This function is not available.
HitList Properties	Customizes the display of the search results area based on functions of Folio Views 4.1.

TABLE OF CONTENTS

When a text window is displayed full screen, the table of contents will appear on the left. The table of contents is a powerful tool to help you navigate the library. In the Scriptures window, it shows testament, book, and chapter. In the Books window, it shows author, book, and chapter. In the References window, it shows book and section.

TO SEE THE TABLE OF CONTENTS:

Click a window's full-screen display button:

NOTE: You can adjust the size of the table of contents by dragging the bar that separates it from the text being displayed.

For example, with the table of contents open in the Books window, you can use the scroll bar to find a book. After you have found the book you want, you can

- Click the closed book icon to expand the book's table of contents and see what it contains. For example, if you click on the icon by "Benson, Ezra Taft," you'll see the individual books by President Benson, such as A *Labor of Love.*
- Click the closed book icon next to an individual book, such as *A Labor of Love.* When you do, you'll see the individual chapters in that book.
- Double-click on the name of the chapter to read the chapter in the text window. For example, if you double-clicked "Setting Apart Blessing," that chapter would open. Other chapters may

have additional book icons you can open to see subsections of the chapter.

TIP: If you double-click any *title* on the list (not the icon), you'll go to the beginning of that item. For example, if you double-clicked *A Labor of Love*, you'd go to the beginning of that book. If you double-clicked "Home Again," you'd go to the beginning of that chapter.

You can also compress the table of contents so you don't see as much. To do so, click the open book icon by any of the table of contents entries.

NOTE: The table of contents is visible only if you have displayed a window full screen.

TIP: Use the table of contents to get a broad overview of a book you may be interested in reading and to find your way around a book.

SEARCHING FROM THE TABLE OF CONTENTS
You can use the table of contents to search a specific book or several books at a time.

 TO SEARCH SPECIFIC BOOKS FROM THE TABLE OF CONTENTS:

1. Display one of the text windows full screen.

2. In the table of contents, click the checkboxes next to the titles of the work or works you want to search.

3. Click the text window with the right mouse button. A pop-up menu will appear.

4. Click **Advanced Search.**

5. Click the checkbox labeled **Checked branches.**

6. In the **Query For** window, type the words you want to search for.

7. Click **OK** to search the works you selected.

TIP: As you type, the Query dialog attempts to complete the word you are typing with a word contained in the library. If the word is correct, press **Enter** and type the next word. If not, finish typing the correct word. Also, as you type in the words you want to find, you can see how many instances of those words are being found. This lets you quickly revise your search—you can type in different words if your first ones are not found or if the search is finding too many matches to be manageable.

ADVANCED SEARCH

You can use Advanced Query to take advantage of the full power of the Folio Views query syntax. If you're familiar with searching using Folio syntax from previous reference libraries, you can use Advanced Query to find information in various ways. If you are not familiar with this type of searching, you will probably want to search using GospeLink's main toolbar as described on pages 77–86.

Advanced Query gives you complete access to the Folio Views query syntax. This syntax helps you focus and refine your searches through the use of Boolean operators, wildcards, proximity operators, and scope limitations.

NOTE: This search will operate only in the active window and the current view. For example, if you select the LDS Authors view in the Books window, that's the only view that will be searched.

 TO PERFORM AN ADVANCED SEARCH:

1. Click the right mouse button in the window and view you want to search. For example, you might click in the Books window and the General Authorities view.

2. Choose **Advanced Search** from the pop-up menu. The Advanced Query dialog appears.

3. Type the words you want to search for, separated by a space or the appropriate operator. Operators are special symbols or words you can use to perform advanced searches. They include certain characters such as *, ?, and %, and certain words such as *and, or,* and *not.*

- You may search by word (not using any specific operators). For example:
  study faith scriptures
- You may search for an exact phrase. Enclose the phrase in quotation marks. For example:
  "faith without works"
- You may use Boolean operators (and, or, not, exclusive or). For example:
  faith and works
  faith or works
  faith not works
  faith xor works

Boolean operators (named after British mathematician George Boole) let you refine a search to focus on more specific or more general information than you could find with a single word or phrase. Boolean operators require a word or phrase on either side of the operator. For example, "faith or works" is a valid search, but "or faith works" is not. (An exception is the *not* operator, which can be used before a term and still be valid. For example, "not faith works" finds the same thing as "faith not works.") There are four Boolean operators: *and, or, not,* and *xor* (exclusive or). Here is an example of each:

faith and works: Finds all paragraphs that contain both *faith* and *works.*

faith or works: Finds all paragraphs that contain either *faith* or *works* or both.

faith not works: Finds all paragraphs that contain *faith* but not *works.*

faith xor works: Finds all paragraphs that contain either *faith* or *works* but not both.

• You may use wildcards (single character, multiple character, word form, synonym). For example:

wor?

work°

work%

work$

Wildcard operators (so named because they can represent anything) let you create a pattern for the kind of words you want to find. The operators can represent a single character, multiple characters, other forms of a word, or synonyms for a word. For example:

wom?n: Finds all words that match the pattern for a single character (such as *woman* or *women*).

work°: Finds all words that match the pattern for multiple characters (such as *work, worked, workhorse,* or *workaholic*).

work%: Finds related forms of the word used in the pattern (such as *work, works, worked,* or *working*).

work$: Finds synonyms of the word used in the pattern (such as *toil, effort,* or *trade*).

• You may use proximity operators to specify how close terms must be. For example:

"faith"/5

Proximity operators let you specify how close two (or more) words must be to each other before your search will find them. For example:

"faith works"/5: Finds paragraphs that contain *faith* and *works*, in that order, within a five-word range.

"faith works"@8: Finds paragraphs that contain *faith* and *works*, in any order, within an eight-word range.

"faith works"#3: Finds paragraphs that contain *faith* and *works*, in any order, within three paragraphs of each other.

If you want to modify a previous query, click the **Prev** button next to the **Query For** box to display the previous query.

Note that as you type, the Query dialog attempts to complete the word you are typing with a word contained in the library. If the word is correct, press **Enter** and type the next word.

Queries may be as many as 2,048 characters in length.

4. Click **OK** to apply the search to the current window and view.

Advanced Search Syntax

The following table lists and gives examples of the various operators that can be used with the Folio software and thus with GospeLink. The operators may look intimidating, but they can be very useful in finding exactly what you're looking for. You can get more information on advanced searching by starting Folio Views 4.1 (see page 11) and clicking the Help menu.

Operator or Scope	Example
And	one two — one & two — one and two
Or	me | you, me or you
Not	^him — not him — her ^ him
Exclusive Or (Xor)	apples ~ oranges — apples xor oranges
Phrase	"to be or not" — "fourscore and seven"
Single Character Wildcard	wom?n — g??b?r
Multiple Character Wildcard	work° — h°t°
Ordered Proximity	"united states of america"/10
Unordered Proximity	"uncle sams army"@7
Record Proximity	"smith jones theft deny"#5
Stem (Word Form)	run% — great%
Thesaurus (Synonym)	flying$ — alterations$
Contents	Contents Old Testament,Genesis] noah and ark
Partition	[Partition Chapter] advanced query
Rank	[Rank 10] dogs chase cats
Fields	Field judge: scalia]
Range	[Field weapons: > .357 < .45]
Highlighters	[Highlighter humor: marx | stooge]

Pop-ups and Notes	Note words to find] or [Pop-up my favorite feature]
Groups	[Group animals] warthog lion rat
Headings	[Heading <level name>,<heading path>: query]
Levels	Level <level name>: <query>]

COPYING

When you're using the text windows, GospeLink lets you copy text to several locations. This gives you great flexibility, whether you use your own word processor or Composer, the word processor included with GospeLink.

PLACES TEXT CAN BE COPIED

Clipboard	The standard Windows Clipboard. Copy text here if you would like to paste it into your regular word processor.
Composer	A basic word processor included with GospeLink. You can copy text directly to Composer without pasting.
PrePrint	A place to collect items you want to print. GospeLink lets you copy many text selections, organize or delete them, and then print them all at once. You can also copy items from PrePrint to the Windows Clipboard, Composer, or your PalmPilot.
PalmPilot	A "personal digital assistant" from 3Com. GospeLink lets you copy text to a file that you can download to your PalmPilot.

WAYS TO COPY

GospeLink gives you three different ways to copy text:
- Standard Windows copy command (**Ctrl+C**)

- **Copy to . . .** on the pop-up menus
- **Copy To** on the drop-down menus

 TO COPY WITH THE STANDARD WINDOWS COPY COMMAND (CTRL+C):

1. Select the text you want to copy.
2. Hold down the **Ctrl** key.
3. Press the **C** key.

The selected text will be copied to the Windows Clipboard, and you can paste it into your word processor.

 TO COPY WITH "COPY TO . . . " ON A POP-UP MENU:

1. Select the text you want to copy, or just place your cursor in a paragraph you want to copy. This selects the whole paragraph, making selection easy and fast.
2. Click the text window with the right mouse button.
3. On the pop-up menu, click **Copy to . . .**
4. Choose the copy option that meets your needs. You can copy to the Windows Clipboard, Composer, PrePrint, or your PalmPilot.

 TO COPY WITH "COPY TO" ON A DROP-DOWN MENU:

1. Select the text you want to copy, or just place your cursor in a paragraph you want to copy. This selects the whole paragraph, making selection easy and fast.
2. Click the down arrow in the top left corner of a text window.
3. On the drop-down menu, click **Copy To.**
4. The Copy To window will appear.
5. Choose the option that meets your needs. You can copy to the Windows Clipboard, Composer, PrePrint, or your PalmPilot.

If you select **Copy To** from a drop-down menu, you'll see the window shown above. This window lets you copy information from the library into different formats and places.

Currently selected text will be displayed on the left. If text is not selected, you'll see the text where your cursor (not the mouse pointer) is located.

NOTE: The selection includes whole paragraphs, making selection easy and fast.

Choose the option that meets your needs. You can copy the displayed text into the Windows Clipboard, Composer, PrePrint, or your PalmPilot.

Copy text to Clipboard	Copies text to the Windows Clipboard. Use this option if you want to paste the text into your regular word processor.
Copy text to Composer	Copies text directly to Composer, GospeLink's built-in word processor.

Copy text to PrePrint	Copies text to PrePrint.
Copy text to PalmPilot	Copies text to a file you can download to your PalmPilot.

COPY OPTIONS

You can set two options—Include reference lines and Include source—to determine what is included with the copied text.

Include Reference Lines	Includes reference lines above each paragraph being copied. These reference lines indicate where each paragraph was copied from.
Include Source	Includes the source of the text copied. The source will appear at the end of the copied text. **WARNING!** This option may not work correctly if your selection includes text from more than one book.

 TO COPY TEXT TO THE WINDOWS CLIPBOARD:

1. Select the text you want to copy.
2. Click the down arrow in the top left corner of a text window.
3. Click **Copy To.** The copy menu will appear.
4. Click **Copy text to Clipboard.**

The text will be copied to the Windows Clipboard, and a message will appear notifying you that this has taken place.

 TO COPY TEXT TO COMPOSER:

1. Select the text you want to copy.
2. Click the down arrow in the top left corner of a text window.
3. Click **Copy To.** The copy menu will appear.
4. Click **Copy text to Composer.**

If Composer is open, the text will be copied directly to it. If not, Composer will start and the text will be copied to it.

 TO COPY TEXT TO PREPRINT:

1. Select the text you want to copy.
2. Click the down arrow in the top left corner of a text window.

3. Click **Copy To.** The copy menu will appear.

4. Click **Copy text to PrePrint.**

If PrePrint is open, the text will be copied directly to it. If not, PrePrint will start and the text will be copied to it.

 TO COPY TEXT TO YOUR PALMPILOT:

1. Select the text you want to copy.

2. Click the down arrow in the top left corner of a text window.

3. Click **Copy To.** The copy menu will appear.

4. Click **Copy text to PalmPilot.**

A dialog box will appear so you can name the document that will be copied to your PalmPilot.

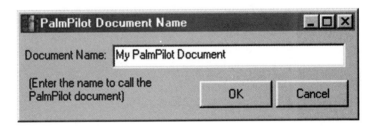

The name you give the document will appear on your PalmPilot, so it should reflect the contents of what is being copied.

GospeLink will then display a standard Windows Save dialog box so you can name the file and specify its location. Then you can download the file to your PalmPilot.

NOTE: You'll need to install the AportisDoc Reader on your PalmPilot in order to copy files to your PalmPilot. (You can also use other PalmPilot doc readers.) For instructions on how to do this, see the **readme** file in the **Palm** folder on your Installation Disk. Also, see your PalmPilot documentation for instructions on downloading files to your PalmPilot.

CHAPTER 4
SCRIPTURES WINDOW

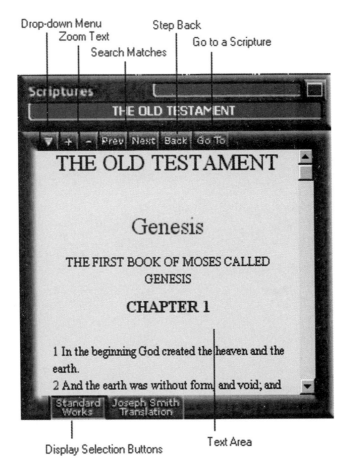

Drop-down Menu
Zoom Text
Search Matches
Step Back
Go to a Scripture

Display Selection Buttons
Text Area

The Scriptures window is on the left side of GospeLink's main window. It displays the standard works and the Joseph Smith Translation of the Bible. The standard works include the full text of the Old Testament, New Testament, Book of Mormon, Doctrine and Covenants, and Pearl of Great Price. You can use the Scriptures window to study the scriptures, and if you click a hypertext scripture reference in one of the other windows, it will take you to that scripture in the Scriptures window.

The Scriptures window works like the other text windows in GospeLink. You can scroll through the text, search for specific information, copy text, print text, make notes, highlight, place bookmarks, go to specific references, resize the text, and so on. This table shows the functions of the buttons in the Scriptures window:

Drop-down menu	You can activate the drop-down menu by clicking the down arrow in the upper left corner of the Scriptures window. This menu lets you copy text, send selections to PrePrint, place a bookmark, highlight text, erase highlights, save your work, and undo the last few things you've done.
+ and − (change text size)	The + and − buttons change the size of the text. Clicking the + button makes text bigger for easier reading. Clicking the − button makes text smaller for easy overview and selection.
Prev and Next	After you've performed a search, the Prev and Next buttons let you move from one match, or "hit," to another. The Next button moves to the next match, and the Prev button moves to the previous match.
Back	This button takes you back to the previous hypertext link or the previous search.
Go To	The Go To button activates the Scripture Guide, which you can use to go quickly to a specific verse of scripture.
Text area	The text area displays the text of the scriptures.

Display selection buttons	The display selection buttons change what you see in the Scriptures window: • Click the first button to see the standard works. • Click the second button to see the Joseph Smith Translation.
Pop-up menus	If you click the right mouse button in the text area, a pop-up menu will appear. This menu gives you a quick way to copy, print, search, place a bookmark, and highlight text.

SIDE-BY-SIDE COMPARISONS

GospeLink lets you see the scriptures side by side with other books for truly effective gospel study. When you first start GospeLink, you'll see the Scriptures window, the Books window, and the References window all at the same time. However, you can hide the References window to see the Scriptures window and the Books window in a true side-by-side comparison.

TO HIDE THE REFERENCES WINDOW:

Click the References window's first display button:

STUDYING THE SCRIPTURES SIDE BY SIDE

You can also use both the Scriptures window and the Books window to display the scriptures, so that you can read the scriptures in a true side-by-side comparison. This is especially useful if you're studying the scriptures and want to keep your place in one verse while reading other verses at the same time. You can have the Book of Mormon open next to the Bible, the Bible open next to the Doctrine and Covenants, or any other combination.

TO SEE THE SCRIPTURES SIDE BY SIDE:

1. Start the Scripture Guide by clicking the **Go To** button at the top of the Scriptures window:

2. The Scripture Guide will appear:

3. Click the **Start side-by-side comparison** button. The scriptures will be displayed in the Books window as well as in the Scriptures window.

At this point, you'll see two new options on the Scripture Guide: Left Window and Right Window:

These options let you choose the window that will display the scriptures you specify in the Scripture Guide:

Left Window	Displays the selected Scripture Guide reference in the Scriptures window.
Right Window	Displays the selected Scripture Guide reference in the Books window.

The Scripture Guide will remain open on your screen, and you can continue to use it to see different verses in the window of your choice. Or you can close the Scripture Guide but continue to display the side-by-side comparison; just click the **Close** button.

COMPARING THE KING JAMES VERSION WITH THE JOSEPH SMITH TRANSLATION

You can also study the King James Version of the Bible side by side with the Joseph Smith Translation. This lets you compare the translations to see Joseph Smith's inspired changes.

 TO COMPARE THE KJV WITH THE JST:

1. Start the side-by-side comparison of the scriptures as explained above.

2. Click the Joseph Smith Translation button at the bottom of the Scriptures window:

You'll see the Joseph Smith Translation in the Scriptures window and the King James Version in the Books window. As an additional feature when you compare the JST with the KJV, the two versions are automatically synchronized. So as you move through the King James Version, the Joseph Smith Translation will automatically move with you.

- If you place your cursor in a verse of the King James Version, you'll see the corresponding verse in the JST at the *top* of the Scriptures window.
- It is the content of the verses, not necessarily the verse numbering, that is synchronized. The JST verse numbers don't always correspond with the King James Version because Joseph Smith added verses to the biblical record.
- If you place your cursor in a verse of the JST and move through it, the standard works will *not* move with you. This lets you move through the JST independently if you need to, but still synchronize the verses when you move back to the KJV.
- The JST text is displayed in blue to distinguish it from the KJV.

ENDING SIDE-BY-SIDE COMPARISON

 TO END SIDE-BY-SIDE COMPARISON:

1. Display the Scripture Guide by clicking the **Go To** button at the top of the Scriptures window.

2. Click the **Stop side-by-side comparison** button:

Or, click the **Close Scripture Compare** button at the bottom of the Books window:

Close Scripture Compare

The Books window will return to the way you left it.

PARALLEL PASSAGES

Another important side-by-side comparison of the scriptures is parallel passages. With GospeLink, you can automatically compare parallel passages in the following:

- The King James Version and the Joseph Smith Translation.
- The creation account in Genesis and the creation accounts in the books of Moses and Abraham (Genesis 1; Moses 2; Abraham 4).
- The Sermon on the Mount in the New Testament and the Sermon at the Temple in the Book of Mormon (Matthew 5–7; 3 Nephi 12–14).
- The book of Isaiah in the Bible and the Isaiah passages in the Book of Mormon (such as Isaiah 2–14; 2 Nephi 12–24).
- Other miscellaneous scriptures.

 TO SEE PARALLEL PASSAGES IN THE SCRIPTURES:

1. In the Scriptures window, click a verse from one of the passages mentioned above.

2. In the References window, click the **Cross-References** button.

3. Look at the references under the heading **"The following verses have similar text."**

4. Click a reference you are interested in seeing.

The parallel verse will be displayed at the *top* of the Books window.

TO END PARALLEL PASSAGES:

1. Display the Scripture Guide.
2. Click the **Stop side-by-side comparison** button:

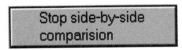

Or, click the **Close Scripture Compare** button at the bottom of the Books window:

The Books window will return to the way you left it.

SCRIPTURE GUIDE

Scripture Guide is a quick way of going directly to a scripture. You can leave Scripture Guide open on your screen while reading the scriptures you select in the Scriptures window.

Scripture Guide also lets you see the scriptures side by side in the Scriptures window and the Books window at the same time.

 TO START SCRIPTURE GUIDE:

To start Scripture Guide, click the **Go To** button on the Scriptures window.

Click the Go To button
on the Scriptures Window

TO FIND A SCRIPTURE WITH SCRIPTURE GUIDE:

Select a book of scripture in the book list, which looks like this:

The book list contains all of the books in the standard works listed in alphabetical order. This allows you to select a book without knowing where in the standard works it appears. There are several ways to browse the list:

- Press your up and down cursor keys to go from one book to another.
- Press the first letter of the book you are looking for. For example, pressing **M** will take you to the book of Malachi in the list. If you press **M** again, the book of Mark will be selected.
- Click on the down arrow next to the box to display all the books in the list. Use the scroll bar to move through them. Then click the book you want to select.

After you've selected a book, the Chapter and Verse boxes will contain a list of numbers for you to choose from. Select a chapter or verse in the same way you selected a book. You can also type in the numbers for the chapter and verse you are looking for. Scripture Guide will not allow you to enter a reference that does not exist.

NOTE: Scripture Guide will automatically change the Scriptures window as you make your selections. You'll need the **Go To** button only if you've typed in the reference information.

CHAPTER 5
BOOKS WINDOW

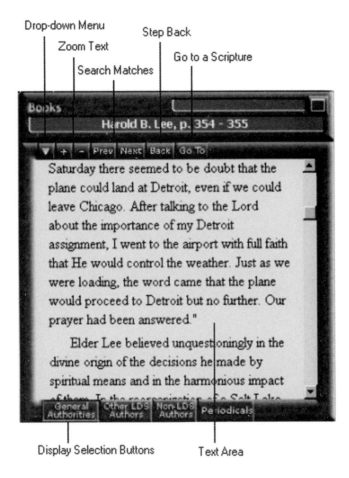

Drop-down Menu

Zoom Text

Search Matches

Step Back

Go to a Scripture

Books

Harold B. Lee, p. 354 - 355

▼ + − Prev Next Back Go To

Saturday there seemed to be doubt that the plane could land at Detroit, even if we could leave Chicago. After talking to the Lord about the importance of my Detroit assignment, I went to the airport with full faith that He would control the weather. Just as we were loading, the word came that the plane would proceed to Detroit but no further. Our prayer had been answered."

Elder Lee believed unquestioningly in the divine origin of the decisions he made by spiritual means and in the harmonious impact

General Authorities   Other LDS Authors   Non-LDS Authors   Periodicals

Display Selection Buttons

Text Area

The Books window is on the right side of GospeLink's main window. It displays all of the works in the GospeLink library except the scriptures and the reference works, which appear in the other two windows.

By clicking the display selection buttons at the bottom of the window, you can display four different kinds of works: works by

General Authorities, works by other LDS authors, works by non-LDS Authors, and periodicals.

The Books window works like the other text display windows in GospeLink. You can scroll through the text, search for specific information, copy text, print text, make notes, highlight, place bookmarks, go to a specific page, resize the text, and so on. This table shows the functions of the buttons in the Books window:

Drop-down menu	You can see the drop-down menu by clicking the down arrow in the upper left corner of the Books window. This menu lets you copy text, send selections to PrePrint, place a bookmark, highlight text, erase highlights, save your work, and undo the last few things you've done.
+ and – (change text size)	The + and – buttons change the size of the text. Clicking the + button makes text bigger for easier reading. Clicking the – button makes text smaller for easy overview and selection.
Prev and Next	After you have performed a search, the Prev and Next buttons let you move from one match, or "hit," to another. The Next button moves to the next match, and the Prev button moves to the previous match.
Back	This button takes you back to the previous hypertext link or to the previous search.
Go To	The Go To button activates the Book Guide, which will take you quickly to a specific page in a book.
Text area	The text area displays the text of the books.

Display selection buttons	The display selection buttons change what you see in the Books window. • Click the first button to see works by General Authorities. • Click the second button to see works by other LDS authors. • Click the third button to see works by non-LDS authors. These are primarily on Disk B in the World Classics Library. • Click the fourth button to see Church periodicals.
Pop-up menus	If you click the right mouse button in the text area, a pop-up menu will appear. This menu gives you a quick way to copy, print, search, place a bookmark, and highlight text.

BOOK GUIDE

Book Guide is a quick way of going directly to a book or a page number in a book. You can leave Book Guide open on your screen while reading the books and pages you select in the Books window.

NOTE: Book Guide lists only books on the current disk. For example, if Disk A is in your CD-ROM drive, only the books on Disk A will be listed.

TO START BOOK GUIDE:

To start Book Guide, click the **Go To** button on the Books window.

Click the Go To
button on the
Books Window

 TO FIND A BOOK AND PAGE WITH BOOK GUIDE:

Select a book from the list of books. This list displays the books in alphabetical order. There are several ways to browse the list:

- Press your up and down cursor keys to go from one book to another.
- Press the first letter of the book you are looking for. For example, pressing **M** will take you to *Making Your Home a Missionary Training Center*, the first book starting with M in the list. If you press **M** again, the second book starting with M, *Man May Know for Himself*, will be selected.
- Click on the down arrow next to the box to display all the books in the list. Use the scroll bar to move through them. Then click the book you want to select.

After you have selected a book, you can type in the number of the page you want to read. Click **Go to** to go to the book and page you have selected. If you do not select a page number, Book Guide will take you to the first page in the book you have selected.

NOTE: Books in the World Classics Library are public domain editions without page numbers.

CHAPTER 6
REFERENCES WINDOW

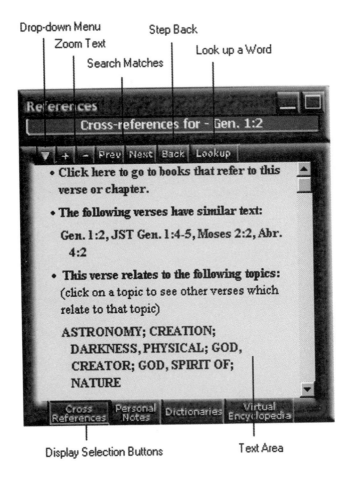

The References window is on the left side of GospeLink's main window, directly under the Scriptures window. It displays reference works and links to information that can be used with text in the other two windows. The References window is navigated with the four main buttons at the bottom of the window: Cross-References, Personal Notes, Dictionaries, and Virtual Encyclopedia. Many reference works were incorporated into the References window to provide valuable information. These works include *Dictionary of the Book of Mormon, Easton's Bible Dictionary, Smith's Bible Dictionary, LDS Virtual Encyclopedia, Strong's Greek Dictionary, Strong's Hebrew Dictionary, A Topical Guide to the Scriptures* (1977), and Webster's 1828 *American Dictionary of the English Language.*

The References window is different from the Scriptures window and the Books window; its main purpose is to show reference material that clarifies information in those windows. For example, if you are in the Scriptures window, the Cross-References view in the References window will display scriptures, books, and topics related to the verse you are studying. The dictionaries and lexicons in the References window provide definitions for words in the other windows. For example, *Webster's 1828 Dictionary* shows the definition of words as they were used in Joseph Smith's time.

The References window also displays your personal notes.

In the References window, you can scroll through the references, copy text, print text, make notes, highlight, place bookmarks, resize text, look up words, and so on. This table shows the functions of the buttons in the References window:

Drop-down menu	You can see the drop-down menu by clicking the down arrow in the upper left corner of the References window. This menu lets you copy text, send selections to PrePrint, place a bookmark, highlight text, erase highlights, save your work, and undo the last few things you've done.
+ and – (change text size)	The + and – buttons change the size of the text. Clicking the + button makes text bigger for easier reading. Clicking the – button makes text smaller for easy overview and selection.
Prev and Next	After you have performed a search, the Prev and Next buttons let you move from one match, or "hit," to another. The Next button moves to the next match, and the Prev button moves to the previous match.

Back	This button takes you back to the previous hypertext link or search.
Lookup	The Lookup button lets you type in a word or Strong's number to look up in the dictionaries or lexicon. (Strong's numbers are used by scholars to identify words in Greek and Hebrew.)
Text area	The text area displays the text of the reference works.
Display selection buttons	The display selection buttons change what you see in the References window. • Click the first button to see cross-references in the Topical Guide. • Click the second button to make or view personal notes. • Click the third button to see dictionary entries. • Click the fourth button to see entries in the *LDS Virtual Encyclopedia.*
Pop-up menus	If you click the right mouse button in the text area, a pop-up menu will appear. This menu gives you a quick way to copy, print, search, place a bookmark, and highlight text.

LOOKING UP A WORD

There are two ways to look up a word in GospeLink's reference works. You can double-click a word or you can click the **Lookup** button.

 DOUBLE-CLICK A WORD:

You can look up any word in the text windows by double-clicking it. The word will be searched for in all of the reference works and displayed in the References window.

CLICK THE LOOKUP BUTTON:

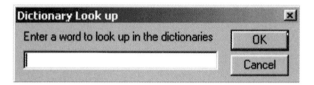

When you click the **Lookup** button, a dialog box will appear, allowing you to type in the word you want to look up. The word will be searched for in all of the reference works and displayed in the References window.

NOTE: You can also key in a Strong's number to be looked up in *Strong's Greek Dictionary* or *Strong's Hebrew Dictionary.*

CROSS-REFERENCES

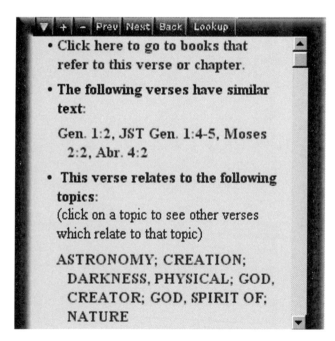

The information in the Cross-References view of the References window is taken from Deseret Book's 1977 *Topical Guide to the Scriptures*. As you scroll through scriptures in the Scriptures window, the cross-references information will change to display pertinent information for the verse your cursor is in. Also, if you click on a verse, information for that verse will be displayed in the Cross-References window.

"THIS VERSE RELATES TO THE FOLLOWING TOPICS"

As you study the scriptures, if you see a topic that looks interesting in the Cross-References window, you can click it to see all of the other scripture references related to that topic. If you click one of those references, the scripture it refers to will appear in the Scriptures window. This makes it possible to quickly find scriptures that are related to each other by topic. It is similar to using the footnote cross-references in your printed scriptures.

"THE FOLLOWING VERSES HAVE SIMILAR TEXT"

Sometimes in the References window, you'll see the words **"The following verses have similar text,"** followed by a list of scripture references. (This option displays only when this feature is available.) If you click one of those references, it will be displayed in the Books window as a scripture comparison. This makes it possible to compare parallel passages from the scriptures. The parallel passages include:

- The King James Version and the Joseph Smith Translation.
- The creation account in Genesis and the creation accounts in the books of Moses and Abraham.
- The Sermon on the Mount in the New Testament and the Sermon at the Temple in the Book of Mormon.
- The book of Isaiah in the Bible and the Isaiah passages in the Book of Mormon.
- Other miscellaneous scriptures.

For more information on how to use this feature, see Parallel Passages on page 58.

TIP: Sometimes if a verse in the King James Version has significant changes in the Joseph Smith Translation, the following line will appear in the References window: **"See changes to this verse in the JST."** If you click this line, it will take you to the JST verse in the Books window so you can see the changes that were made.

"Click here to go to books that refer to this verse or chapter"

The scriptures are linked to the other works in the library so you can see what General Authorities and others have said about them, making the whole library a comprehensive scripture commentary. To use this feature, click the line that reads **"Click here to go to books that refer to this verse or chapter."** The commentary will appear in the Books window.

NOTE: To see commentary by General Authorities, click the **General Authorities** button; to see commentary by other LDS authors, click the **Other LDS Authors** button; and so on.

Personal Notes

The Personal Notes window is like a pocket notepad. You can use it as a kind of reading journal, to track your progress or to jot down thoughts and ideas as you read.

 To type a personal note:

    1. Click the **Personal Notes** button at the bottom of the References window.

    2. Type your personal note into the References window.

NOTE: The Personal Notes window is not meant to replace your word processor, and it has extremely limited word-processing capability. It's designed for taking brief, unformatted notes. If you want to do more advanced word processing, use GospeLink's Composer or your regular word processor. To create notes attached to specific paragraphs in GospeLink's library, use personal text notes (see pages 38–39).

TO SAVE YOUR PERSONAL NOTES:

1. Click your notes with the right mouse button. A pop-up menu will appear.

2. Click **Save.**

Your notes will be saved to your hard drive and will be available the next time you start GospeLink.

NOTE: You can also save your personal notes by clicking the **Save** button on the main toolbar.

 TO COPY YOUR PERSONAL NOTES TO THE WINDOWS CLIPBOARD:

1. Select the text in your personal notes that you want to copy.

2. Click the text with the right mouse button. A pop-up menu will appear.

3. Click **Copy.**

The text will be saved to the Windows Clipboard. You can then paste it into Composer, your regular word processor, or another Windows application.

 TO DELETE YOUR PERSONAL NOTES:

1. Click your notes with the right mouse button. A pop-up menu will appear.

2. Click **Clear.**

3. Confirm the deletion.

All of your notes will be deleted.

WARNING! Once your notes are deleted, you cannot get them back. Use extreme caution in selecting this option!

DICTIONARIES

The Dictionaries view of the References window includes several dictionaries to help you with your gospel study: *Dictionary of the Book of Mormon,* Webster's 1828 *American Dictionary of the English Language, Easton's Bible Dictionary, Smith's Bible Dictionary, Strong's Greek Dictionary,* and *Strong's Hebrew Dictionary.*

When you double-click a word in a text window, that word will be looked up in all the dictionaries at once. (See "Looking Up a Word" on pages 67–68.) The first dictionary that contains a reference to the word will be displayed in the References window.

To see the word in any of the other dictionaries, click the down arrow at the left of the reference box in the References window:

The list of dictionaries will be displayed. Those with a red dot contain the word you looked up.

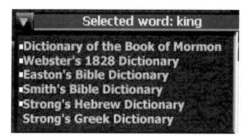

To see what a dictionary has to say about the word, click the name of the dictionary with the mouse. The definition from that dictionary will appear in the References window.

You can also use the **Prev** and **Next** buttons to scroll through the dictionaries for every occurrence of the word you looked up.

LDS VIRTUAL ENCYCLOPEDIA

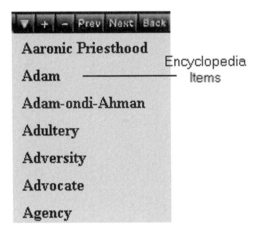

GospeLink's *LDS Virtual Encyclopedia* is a selection of succinct, informative passages on a wide variety of gospel topics. Passages are taken from the many books in the GospeLink library. If you want to know the basics about a particular subject, this is the place to look.

To use the *LDS Virtual Encyclopedia,* click the **Virtual Encyclopedia** button at the bottom of the References window. A list of topics will appear in alphabetical order, and you can scroll through the list using the scroll bar. To select a topic, click it with the left mouse button. The information on that topic will appear in the Books window, marked with a red line on the left side of the text. You can also learn more about the topic by looking above and below the red line in the book that includes the passage.

The **Next** and **Prev** buttons will scroll through the information in the Books window. For example, if you are looking at works by General Authorities, the buttons will scroll through information by General Authorities on the topic you selected.

NOTE: Information on the topic you selected may appear in works by both General Authorities and other LDS authors. If there is information in the General Authorities view, it will be displayed first. To see information in works by other LDS authors, click the **Other LDS Authors** button below the Books window.

General Authorities	Displays information on your topic written by General Authorities.
Other LDS Authors	Displays information on your topic written by other LDS authors.

PART 3: USING THE MAIN TOOLBAR

CHAPTER 7
MAIN TOOLBAR OVERVIEW

GospeLink's main toolbar is composed of buttons that take you to other windows or that run various features. To select an item from the toolbar, click the button for the feature you want to use. For example, if you click the **Composer** button, you'll start Composer, GospeLink's built-in word processor.

The following table lists each main toolbar button and describes the feature it activates:

Search	Displays GospeLink's Search window, where you can search the GospeLink library in a variety of ways.
Clear Search	Clears a search in all three of GospeLink's text windows.
Explorer	Starts GospeLink Explorer. Explorer is a card catalog for the GospeLink library. You can use Explorer to find information in a variety of ways.

Ensign Index	Displays an index of the *Ensign* magazine by author, title, topic, and feature. You can use the Ensign Index to find articles in the printed *Ensign* magazine. (The actual text of the *Ensign* is not included with GospeLink.)
Composer	Starts GospeLink Composer. Composer is a word processor that includes special functions tied to the GospeLink library. For example, you can copy text from a text window directly into Composer.
Highlight	Lets you create and maintain your own set of highlighters.
Printing	Starts PrePrint, which allows you to select multiple items to be printed and then view the items, rearrange or remove them, and print them. You can also send them to Composer or to a PalmPilot.
Options	Lets you set your own preferences for how GospeLink works.
Tools	Lets you switch disks, change users, reset the text size, and start over.
Help	Starts GospeLink's Online Help system.
Save	Saves new bookmarks, highlighting, and notes.
Exit	Closes the GospeLink program.

CHAPTER 8
SEARCH

GospeLink includes powerful ways to search for specific information, using Folio Views 4.1 as its search engine. It will handle all kinds of searches, from the simplest to the most complex.

 TO OPEN GOSPELINK'S SEARCH WINDOW:

Click the **Search** button on the main toolbar. The Search window will appear:

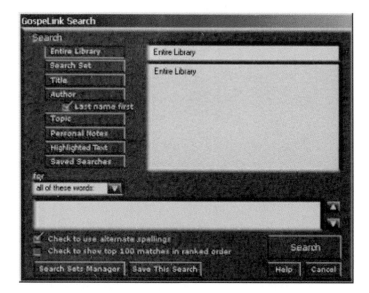

The Search window lets you narrow your searches, making it easier to find the information you need. You can search the entire library, a single title, a single author, or a topic. You can search groups of books, called Search Sets. You can also search personal notes and highlighted text. And you can save a search for use in the future.

SELECTING WHAT TO SEARCH

These buttons on the Search window let you select a category of information you want to search. To search by author, for example, click the **Author** button. The following table shows what each button searches:

Entire Library	Searches the entire GospeLink library.
Search Set	Searches all of the books in a Search Set, which is a specific group of books. GospeLink comes with several predefined Search Sets; you can also create your own.
Title	Searches a specific book.
Author	Searches all of the works by a specific author. (You can sort these by first name or last name.)
Topic	Searches all of the works on a specific topic.
Personal Notes	Searches the personal text notes you've created in various paragraphs in the library text. **NOTE:** This option does not search personal notes in the References window.

Highlighted Text	Searches text you have highlighted. You can search by a specific highlighter or by all of your highlighters.
Saved Searches	Displays a search you have previously performed and saved.

NOTE: The default search is the entire library.

SEARCH SELECTION LIST

Once you have selected the category of information you want to search, the Search Selection List in the window on the right will display the specific items you can search. For example:
- If you select Title, the list will display all the books in the library.
- If you select Author, the list will contain all the authors in the library.
- If you select Search Set, the list will contain the predefined Search Sets and those you have created.

NOTE: When you search Personal Notes, the window on the right will list the different views in which you can search your notes. When you are using Disk A, you can search General Authorities, other LDS Authors, the Joseph Smith Translation, and the standard works. With Disk B, you can search Non-LDS Authors, Periodicals, the Joseph Smith Translation, and the standard works.

 TO SELECT AN ITEM FROM THE LIST:

Use your cursor keys and your **Page Up** and **Page Down** keys to scroll through the list. Then click the specific item you want to search. The item will be highlighted in a different color, and the name of the item will appear at the top of the screen.

After selecting an item (which sets the focus on the list), you can also press a letter key to jump to the first item in the list that begins with that letter. For example, in the list of books, pressing **S** would jump to *Sacred Truths of the Doctrine and Covenants, vol. 1*, the first title in the list beginning with S. If you pressed **S** again, the next item that starts with S would be selected.

You can also use the scroll bar to move through the list.

TIP: Try using the Search Set called "Book and Chapter Titles" to find books and chapters that discuss a specific topic you are interested in. You can use other Search Sets, such as "New Testament" and "Brigham Young," to help find information for teaching Gospel Doctrine, priesthood, and Relief Society classes. The Search Sets for "Old Testament," "New Testament," and so on are collections of books *about* those volumes of scripture, not the scriptures themselves. (For more information on Search Sets, see pages 87– 101.)

SEARCH FOR

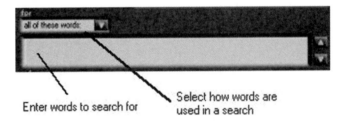

Enter words to search for

Select how words are used in a search

After you've selected what to search, you're ready to tell GospeLink the word, words, or phrase you want to find. First, narrow your search by telling the program what to find depending on how the words are used in a search. To do this, make one of these selections from the **for** box:

all of these words	Searches for paragraphs that contain all of the words you specify. (If you typed in three words to find, paragraphs containing only two of the words would not be included.)
any of these words	Searches for paragraphs that contain any of the words you specify. (If you typed in three words to find, paragraphs containing any one of those words would be included.)

this exact phrase	Searches for paragraphs containing the words you specify in the order you typed them. (If you typed in three words to find, paragraphs containing those three words together, in order, would be included.)

Finally, in the large word box under the **for** box, type in the word, words, or phrase you want GospeLink to find. If you're searching for more than one word, be sure you have selected the kind of search you want in the **for** box.

START A SEARCH

After making all the selections of what to search, how to search, and what to search for, you can start the search by clicking the **Search** button or hitting **Enter**. The results of the search will appear in the text windows.

SEARCH EXAMPLES

 TO SEARCH A BOOK FOR THE WORDS *FAITH* AND *WORKS* USED TOGETHER:

    1. Click the **Search** button on the main toolbar.
    2. Click the **Title** button.
    3. Select the book you want to search (for example, *Believing Christ*).
    4. Select "all of these words" in the **for** box.
    5. Type *faith* and *works* in the word box.
    6. Click the **Search** button or hit **Enter.**

 TO SEARCH AN AUTHOR FOR THE WORDS EITHER *REPENTANCE* OR *CHANGE:*

    1. Click the **Search** button on the main toolbar.
    2. Click the **Author** button.
    3. Select the author you want to search (for example, Ezra Taft Benson).

4. Select "any of these words" in the **for** box.

5. Type *repentance* and *change* in the word box.

6. Click the **Search** button or hit **Enter.**

 TO SEARCH A TOPIC FOR THE PHRASE *FAITH WITHOUT WORKS:*

1. Click the **Search** button on the main toolbar.

2. Click the **Topic** button.

3. Select the topic you want to search (for example, Atonement).

4. Select "this exact phrase" in the **for** box.

5. Type *faith without works* in the word box.

6. Click the **Search** button or hit **Enter.**

 TO SEARCH A SEARCH SET FOR *KING LAMONI:*

1. Click the **Search** button on the main toolbar.

2. Click the **Search Set** button.

3. Select the Search Set you want to use (for example, Book of Mormon Commentaries).

4. Select "this exact phrase" in the **for** box.

5. Type *King Lamoni* in the word box.

6. Click the **Search** button or hit **Enter.**

NUMBER OF MATCHES

If your search finds anything, the number of matches will appear in a display label on the upper right of the text window. For example, the display label might say "1 out of 92." Then, as you scroll through the matches, the label will change to show which match you are seeing: "2 out of 92," "3 out of 92," and so on.

If your search found nothing, you'll see a message notifying you of that fact.

TIP: To see the number of matches *before* you actually do the search, use an advanced search. (To learn more about advanced searching, see pages 44–48.)

SEARCH HISTORY

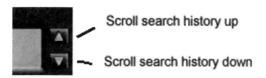

Scroll search history up

Scroll search history down

GospeLink's "search history" remembers all of the searches you perform during a session of GospeLink. That means you can use a search again and again. You can also save searches for use in future GospeLink sessions. If you do not save your searches, they will be lost when you end your GospeLink session.

You can review the searches you have performed by clicking the arrows on the right side of the word box:

▲	Click here to move up through the search history.
▼	Click here to move down through the search history.

If you see a search you want to run again:
1. Select the search by clicking it.
2. Press the **Search** button or hit **Enter.**

TIP: You can also modify a search from the search history. For example, you can add or remove words. You can also change the selection in the **for** box, and you can change the other search options.

SEARCH OPTIONS

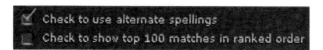

There are two additional search options to help you refine your search. They are searching using alternate spellings and showing the top 100 matches found in ranked order. These options are found to the left of the **Search** button at the bottom of the Search window.

CHECK TO USE ALTERNATE SPELLINGS

When this option is checked, GospeLink includes alternate spellings in its search. This is especially useful in searching the scriptures, which use many alternate spellings. For example, if you search for the word *honor,* GospeLink will also find *honour,* the spelling used in the King James Version. If you search for the word *say,* GospeLink will find *say, sayest,* and *saith.* This option makes it possible to find word variations you might not think of on your own.

CHECK TO SHOW TOP 100 MATCHES IN RANKED ORDER

When this option is checked, GospeLink uses special logic to rank the matches in order from best match to worst. The number of matches is limited to the best 100 and applies only to searches of the entire library.

If the option is not checked, GospeLink ranks the matches in the order it found them in the library. For example, a match found in the Old Testament will be displayed before a match in the New Testament.

SEEING SEARCH MATCHES ONLY

If you want, when you perform a search you can display only the paragraphs containing matches for your search. This option will hide all of the other paragraphs in the books you are searching, which saves you the time of having to scroll through them.

 TO SEE ONLY THE PARAGRAPHS CONTAINING MATCHES FOR YOUR SEARCH:

1. Click the window in which you want to see the matching paragraphs only.

2. Press the *right* mouse button. A pop-up menu will appear.

3. Click **Show Search Results Only.**

Only the paragraphs containing matches for your search will be displayed.

NOTE: This action applies only to the window you selected. The other windows will continue to display all paragraphs.

TO SEE ALL PARAGRAPHS:

1. Click the window in which only the matching paragraphs are displayed.

2. Press the *right* mouse button. A pop-up menu will appear, showing a checkmark next to **Show Search Results Only.** The checkmark indicates that the option is selected.

3. Click **Show Search Results Only** to turn off this option.

All paragraphs in the books you are searching will be displayed.

NOTE: This action applies only to the window you selected.

SAVING SEARCHES

GospeLink lets you save searches for future study sessions. For example, if you started writing a talk on Saturday, you could save your search and turn off your computer. Then you could start your computer on Sunday morning to finish your talk, and you could use the search results from the same search you saved the day before.

 TO SAVE A SEARCH:

1. Click the **Save This Search** button at the bottom middle of the Search window.

2. Enter a name for the search in the box.

3. Click **OK** or press **Enter.**

NOTE: The name must be different from those of other searches you have saved. You should select an appropriate name that will remind you what the search was for.

TIP: You may want to use the words in the search as its name. That way, you'll have no question about what the search was for.

- You can save a search before or after you run it.
- You can find a search in the search history, select it, and save it.

NOTE: Your searches are saved in the search history only during your current session of GospeLink. If you want to use them in a future session, be sure to save them as explained above.

DELETING SEARCHES

 TO DELETE A SEARCH:

1. Click the **Saved Searches** button from the list of search options in the main search window.

2. Click the name of the search you want to delete.

3. Click the **Delete a Search** button at the bottom of the window. (This button replaces the **Save This Search** button when the **Saved Searches** button is clicked.)

CHAPTER 9
SEARCH SETS

Search Sets are collections of books that have been grouped together for searching. GospeLink comes with dozens of predefined Search Sets, including

- Biographies, Autobiographies
- Church History
- Conference Reports
- Doctrine
- Gospel Living
- Improvement Era
- Last Days
- Marriage and Family
- Missionary
- Scripture Commentary
- Teachings of the Prophets

Most of the predefined Search Sets are programmed directly into GospeLink and are available on the **Author** and **Topic** buttons in the Search window. Others (such as Teachings of the Prophets) can be used by clicking the **Search Sets** button in the Search window. You can also create and edit your own Search Sets.

For information on how to search with Search Sets, see page 80.

CREATE A SEARCH SET

 TO CREATE A SEARCH SET:

1. Click the **Search** button on the main toolbar.

2. Click the **Search Sets Manager** button at the bottom left of the Search window.

The Search Sets Manager window will open. This window is the first window of a Wizard, which is a program that will walk you through a process—in this case, creating a Search Set. In each window, follow the instructions in that window and then click the **Next** button to go to the next window. If you change your mind about something, you can click the **Back** button to return to a previous window.

WINDOW 1: SELECT WHAT YOU WANT TO DO

To create a Search Set, click **Create a Search Set.**

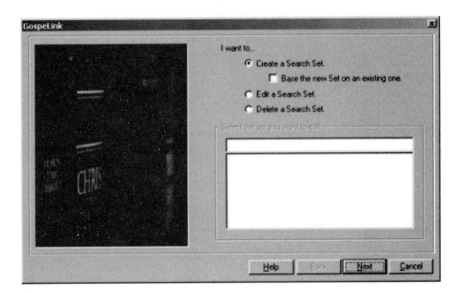

 WINDOW 2: NAME THE SEARCH SET

The second window lets you name your Search Set. Enter a unique name in the box provided.

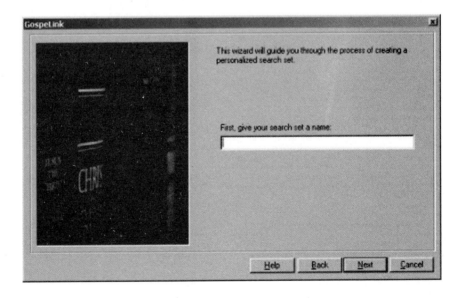

WINDOW 3: SELECT THE BOOKS FOR YOUR SEARCH SET

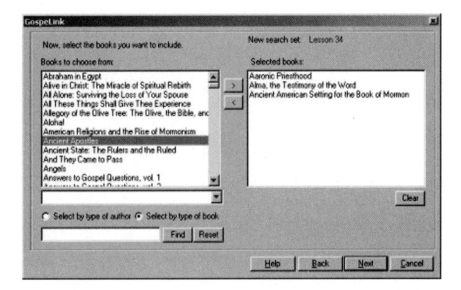

The third window lets you select the books you want to include in your Search Set. On the left is a list of the books in the library. On the right are the books in your Search Set. The arrow buttons in the middle let you add books to or remove books from the right window.

The Book Selection window also provides some tools to narrow the kinds of books you want to see:

Select by type of author	Lets you choose the type of author whose books you want to see. For example, Presidents of the Church, Apostles, Other General Authorities, and so on. If you select this option, only books by the type of author you choose will appear in the list.
Select by type of book	Lets you choose the type of book you want to see. For example, Biography, Doctrinal, Historical, Missionary, Reference, Youth, and so on. If you use this option, only books of the type you select will appear in the list.

Find	Finds book titles that contain the words you enter in this box.
	NOTE: If you have selected a type of author or type of book, you have narrowed your search, and only the titles of books within these parameters will be found. For example, if you select books by Presidents of the Church and search for the word *faith* here, only Church presidents' books whose titles contain the word *faith* will appear.
Reset	Resets the list to include all books.

 BOOKS TO CHOOSE FROM

Use the list of books in the Books to Choose From window to select the books you want in your Search Set. You can select books in the following ways:

Click a book	Click a book to select it.
Click and drag	Click a book, hold down the left mouse button, and drag the mouse pointer down the list to select a range of books.
Click with the Shift key	Click a book, hold down the **Shift** key, and then click another book farther down the list. The whole range of books will be selected.
Click with the Ctrl key	Hold down the **Ctrl** key and click the books you want to include. Only the books you click will be selected.

TO MOVE YOUR SELECTION TO THE SELECTED BOOKS LIST:

After you've selected a book or books, you can move them to the selected books list by clicking the arrow button.

>	Adds selected books to the selected books list.
<	Removes selected books from the selected books list.

After your Search Set is complete, click the **Next** button to return to the Search Sets Manager.

Help	Starts the GospeLink Help system.
Back	Moves back one screen.
Next	Creates the Search Set with the selected books. You will be given a chance to confirm your selection.
Cancel	Ends the Search Set Manager and returns to GospeLink. This button will cancel any changes you have made.

CREATE A SEARCH SET BASED ON ANOTHER SEARCH SET

TO CREATE A SEARCH SET BY MODIFYING AN EXISTING SEARCH SET:

1. Click the **Search** button on the main toolbar.
2. Click the **Search Sets Manager** button at the bottom left of the Search window.

The Search Sets Manager window will open. This window is the first window of a Wizard, which is a program that will walk you through a process—in this case, creating a Search Set. In each window, follow the instructions and then click the **Next** button to go to the next window. If you change your mind about something, you can click the **Back** button to return to a previous window.

WINDOW 1: SELECT WHAT YOU WANT TO DO

To create a Search Set based on another Search Set, click **Create a Search Set** and then click the box labeled **Base the new Set on an existing one.**

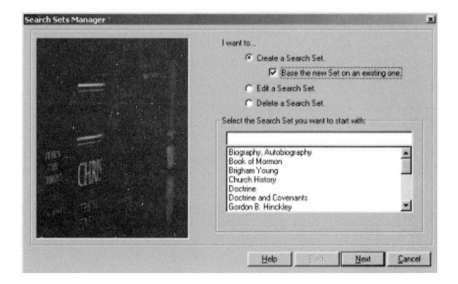

Click the Search Set you want to start with. Then click **Next.**

WINDOW 2: NAME THE SEARCH SET

The second window lets you name your Search Set. Enter a unique name in the box provided. Then click **Next.**

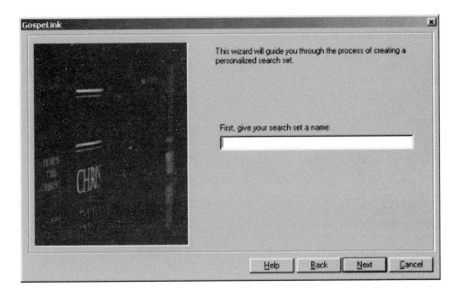

 WINDOW 3: SELECT THE BOOKS FOR YOUR SEARCH SET

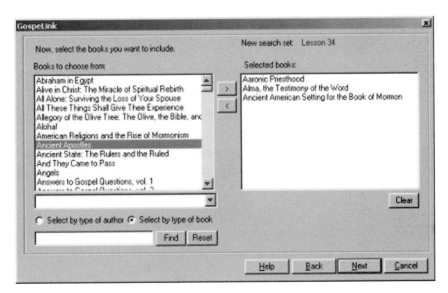

The third window lets you select the books you want to include in your Search Set. On the left is a list of the books in the library. On the right are the books in the existing Search Set you chose. The arrow buttons in the middle let you add books to or remove books from the right window.

The Book Selection window also provides some tools to narrow the kinds of books you want to see:

Select by type of author	Lets you choose the type of author whose books you want to see. For example, Presidents of the Church, Apostles, Other General Authorities, and so on. If you select this option, only books by the type of author you choose will appear in the list.
Select by type of book	Lets you choose the type of book you want to see. For example, Biography, Doctrinal, Historical, Missionary, Reference, Youth, and so on. If you use this option, only books of the type you select will appear in the list.
Find a book	Finds book titles that contain the words you enter in this box. **NOTE:** If you have selected a type of author or type of book, you have narrowed your search, and only the titles of books within these parameters will be found. For example, if you select books by Presidents of the Church and search for the word *faith* here, only Church presidents' books whose titles contain the word *faith* will appear.
Reset	Resets the list to include all books.

TO SELECT THE BOOKS FOR YOUR SEARCH SET:

Use the list of books in the Books to Choose From window to select the books you want in your Search Set. You can select books in the following ways:

Click a book	Click a book to select it.
Click and drag	Click a book, hold down the left mouse button, and drag the mouse pointer down the list to select a range of books.
Click with the shift key	Click a book, hold down the **Shift** key, and then click another book farther down the list. The whole range of books will be selected.
Click with the Ctrl key	Hold down the **Ctrl** key and click the books you want to include. Only the books you click will be selected.

 TO MOVE YOUR SELECTION TO THE SELECTED BOOKS LIST:

After you've selected a book or books, you can move them to the selected books list by clicking the arrow button.

>	Adds selected books to the selected books list.
<	Removes selected books from the selected books list.

After your Search Set is complete, click the **Next** button to return to the Search Sets Manager.

Help	Starts the GospeLink help system.
Back	Moves back one screen.

| Next | Creates the Search Set with the selected books. You will be given a chance to confirm your selection. |
| Cancel | Ends the Search Set Manager and returns to GospeLink. This button will cancel any changes you have made. |

EDIT A SEARCH SET

 TO EDIT A SEARCH SET:

1. Click the **Search** button on the main toolbar.

2. Click the **Search Sets Manager** button at the bottom left of the Search window.

The Search Sets Manager window will open. This window is the first window of a Wizard, which is a program that will walk you through a process—in this case, editing a Search Set. In each window, follow the instructions in that window and then click the **Next** button to go to the next window. If you change your mind about something, you can click the **Back** button to return to a previous window.

WINDOW 1: SELECT WHAT YOU WANT TO DO

To edit a Search Set, click the button labeled **Edit a Search Set.**

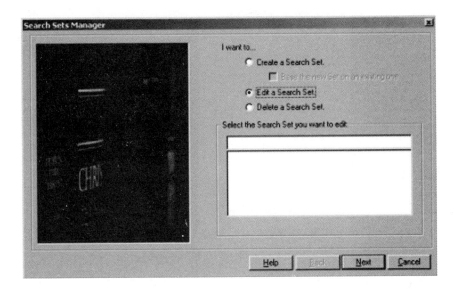

The names of the available Search Sets will appear in the window at the bottom of the screen. Click the Search Set you want to edit. Then click **Next.**

WINDOW 2: SELECT THE BOOKS FOR YOUR SEARCH SET

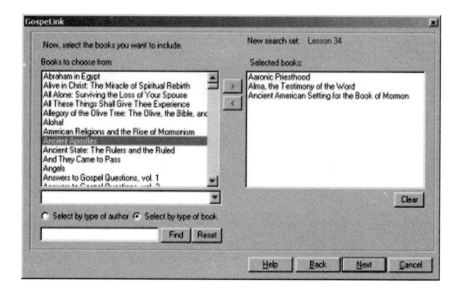

The next window lets you change the books in the Search Set you are editing. On the left is a list of the books in the library. On the right are the books in your Search Set. The arrow buttons in the middle let you add books to or remove books from the right window.

The Book Selection window also provides some tools to narrow the kinds of books you want to see:

Select by type of author	Lets you choose the type of author whose books you want to see. For example, Presidents of the Church, Apostles, Other General Authorities, and so on. If you select this option, only books by the type of author you choose will appear in the list.
Select by type of book	Lets you choose the type of book you want to be see. For example, Biography, Doctrinal, Historical, Missionary, Reference, Youth, and so on. If you use this option, only books of the type you select will appear in the list.

Find	Finds book titles that contain the words you enter in this box.
	NOTE: If you've selected a type of author or type of book, you have narrowed your search, and only the titles of books within these parameters will be found. For example, if you select books by Presidents of the Church and search for the word *faith* here, only Church presidents' books whose titles contain the word *faith* will appear.
Reset	Resets the list to include all books.

 TO SELECT BOOKS:

Use the list of books to select the books you want in your Search Set. You can select books in the following ways:

Click a book	Click a book to select it.
Click and drag	Click a book, hold down the left mouse button, and drag the mouse pointer down the list to select a range of books.
Click with the shift key	Click a book, hold down the **Shift** key, and then click another book farther down the list. The whole range of books will be selected.
Click with the Ctrl key	Hold down the **Ctrl** key and click the books you want to include. Only the books you click will be selected.

TO MOVE YOUR SELECTION TO THE SELECTED BOOKS LIST:

After you've selected a book or books, you can move them to the selected books list by clicking the arrow button.

>	Adds selected books to the selected books list.
<	Removes selected books from the selected books list.

After your Search Set is complete, click the **Next** button to finish editing your Search Set and return to the Search Sets Manager.

Help	Starts the GospeLink Help system.
Back	Moves back one screen.
Next	Creates the Search Set with the selected books. You will be given a chance to confirm your selection.
Cancel	Ends the Search Set Manager and returns to GospeLink. This button will cancel any changes you have made.

DELETE A SEARCH SET

 TO DELETE A SEARCH SET:

1. Click the **Search** button on the main toolbar.
2. Click the **Search Sets Manager** button at the bottom left of the Search window. The Search Sets Manager will open.

3. Click **Delete a Search Set.**

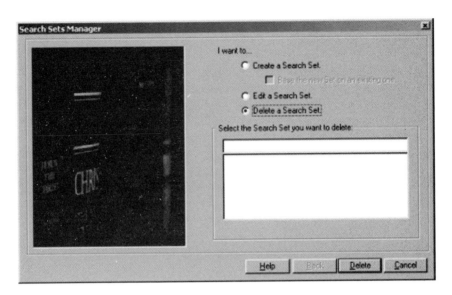

The names of the available Search Sets will appear in the window at the bottom of the screen.

4. Click the Search Set you want to delete.

5. Click **Next.**

A message similar to this one will appear:

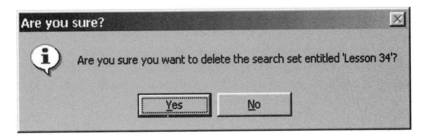

- Click **Yes** to delete the Search Set and return to the Search Sets Manager.
- Click **No** to return to the Search Sets Manager without deleting the Search Set.

CHAPTER 10
CLEAR SEARCH

To clear a search, click the **Clear Search** button on the main toolbar. This will clear all searches in all windows. The matched words will no longer be marked, and the text windows will return to their normal state, with the Search Results window closed.

NOTE: To clear only the searches in a specific window, use the **Clear Search** option available on the pop-up menu by clicking the right mouse button.

CHAPTER 11
GOSPELINK EXPLORER

GospeLink contains a massive amount of information—everything from doctrine to self-help, from biography to history, from ancient philosophy to modern prophecy. This enormous collection would be difficult to manage without a powerful tool like GospeLink Explorer. GospeLink Explorer is like the card catalog in a giant library, only smarter. It lets you explore the information on GospeLink in a variety of ways. It's the place to start when you have a lesson or talk to prepare. GospeLink Explorer is also a great place just to browse the library.

The GospeLink Explorer window is a separate window from GospeLink's text windows. Nevertheless, what you do in GospeLink Explorer affects the text windows. For example, you could use GospeLink Explorer's Books tab to find a book and open it in the Books window. Similarly, you could use the Scriptures tab to find a scripture and open it in the Scriptures window.

NOTE: If your computer is set to a low resolution like 640 x 480, GospeLink Explorer will cover most of the screen. To see more of the screen behind GospeLink Explorer, set your screen resolution to 800 x 600 or higher. To hide GospeLink Explorer, click the **Close** button at the bottom of the window. The next time you open GospeLink Explorer, it will take you back to the same tab and selection you were using before.

GOSPELINK EXPLORER TABS

GospeLink Explorer consists of ten different parts, represented by tabs at the top of the GospeLink Explorer window. Each tab displays a window where you can explore GospeLink in different ways to find the information you need.

To display the window for each tab, simply click it with the mouse. The tabs are grouped together by what they explore:

- To explore the scriptures, use **Scriptures** and **Topics.**
- To explore books, use **Books, Authors, Subjects,** and **Index.**
- To explore talks, use **Talks** and **Speakers.**
- To explore stories and poems, use **Stories/Poems.**
- To explore periodicals, use **Periodicals.**

The following table shows what you can explore using each tab:

What to explore	Tab	Description
Scriptures	Scriptures	Use this tab to: • Go to a scripture. • Select scriptures for printing. • Copy scriptures to the Clipboard. • Copy scriptures to Composer. • Copy scriptures to your PalmPilot. • Find a scripture using Scripture Sets. • Search all of the scriptures, a volume of scripture (such as the Book of Mormon), or a specific book of scripture (such as 1 Nephi).
Scripture Topics	Topics	Use this tab to: • Find scriptures on a specific topic. • Search for a specific topic.

Books	Books	Use this tab to: • List all books alphabetically. • List books by type (biographical, historical, scholarly, inspirational, and so on). • Find a book by words in its title. • Read information about a book. • Read information about a book's author. • Search the text of a selected book or of all books.
Authors of Books	Authors	Use this tab to: • List all authors alphabetically. • List authors by type (President of the Church, Counselor to the President, Apostle, and so on). • Display a list of books by a specific author. • Search the text of books by a specific author or all authors.
Subjects of Books	Subjects	Use this tab to: • Find books on a specific subject. • Search the text of a book on a specific subject.

Indexes of Books	**Index**	Use this tab to: • Look up index entries in the Comprehensive Index, which contains indexes from the LDS books in GospeLink. • Jump from an index entry to the book itself. • Find a book that discusses a certain topic. • Search the Comprehensive Index.
Talks	**Talks**	Use this tab to: • List all talks alphabetically. • List talks by type (talks on faith, hope, charity, and so on). • Find a talk by words in its title. • See a preview of the talk. • Search a selected talk or all talks.
Speakers	**Speakers**	Use this tab to: • List all speakers alphabetically. • List speakers by type (President of the Church, Counselor to the President, Apostle, and so on). • Find talks by a specific speaker. • Find talks by a specific speaker on a specific topic. • Search talks by a selected speaker or all speakers.

Stories/ Poems	Stories/Poems	Use this tab to: • Display a list of poems and stories. • Display a list of authors of these works. • Preview a selected poem or story.
Periodicals	Periodicals	Use this tab to: • Display a list of periodicals and navigate through them. • Select a specific periodical. • Select a specific issue of a periodical. • Search a periodical, a specific issue of a periodical, or all of the periodicals.

CHAPTER 12
SCRIPTURE EXPLORER

Use Scripture Explorer as a quick and easy way to find a scripture reference, search the scriptures, or simply browse the scriptures. You can also use it to find a wide variety of scripture stories, parables, and miracles to use in lessons or talks.

 TO START SCRIPTURE EXPLORER:

1. Click the **Explorer** button on the main toolbar.
2. Click the **Scriptures** tab.

SELECTING A VOLUME OF SCRIPTURE

On the top left of the Scripture Explorer window, select which volume of the standard works you'd like to use: Old Testament, New Testament, Book of Mormon, Doctrine and Covenants, or Pearl of Great Price.

To select a volume, click it with the mouse. The **Select a Book** list will then display the individual books included in that volume of the standard works.

For example, to select the Book of Mormon, click the **Book of Mormon** button. The list of books will then display the books in the Book of Mormon.

NOTE: If you select **All Scriptures,** the box will display all of the books in the standard works.

SELECTING A BOOK

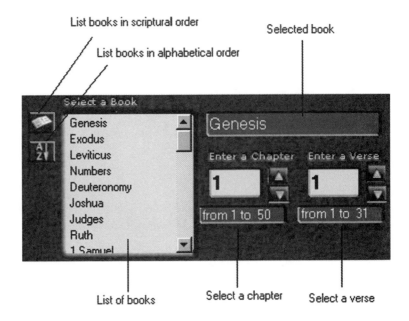

List books in scriptural order

List books in alphabetical order

Selected book

List of books

Select a chapter

Select a verse

In the **Select a Book** list, you can select an individual book of scripture, such as 1 Nephi, Matthew, Isaiah, or Abraham. To do so, click the book you are interested in. The name of the book will appear in the selection label on the upper right. (Sections of the Doctrine and Covenants are treated as chapters and will not be found here.)

You can see the books in their scriptural order (the default view) or in alphabetical order. The following button sorts the books in their scriptural order:

In other words, it lists them as they appear in the standard works. For example, the list of books for the Old Testament starts with Genesis and ends with Malachi.

This button sorts the list alphabetically:

Books starting with numbers, like 1 Chronicles, appear first, followed by the rest of the books in alphabetical order.

TIP: Sorting books alphabetically is especially useful if you're not sure where a book falls in the standard works or if you just want to find it without thinking about where it falls.

SELECTING A CHAPTER AND VERSE

These two boxes let you enter the chapter and verse of the scripture you want to see.

ENTER A CHAPTER

The **Enter a Chapter** box displays the first chapter of the selected book. The label below the box displays the total number of chapters in the book. You can type in the chapter (or section) number you want, or you can click on the arrows to go to a higher or lower chapter number. (GospeLink won't let you select a chapter number that doesn't exist.)

ENTER A VERSE

The **Enter a Verse** box displays the first verse of the selected chapter or section. The text below the box displays the total number of verses in the chapter. You can type in the verse number you want, or you can click on the arrows to go to a higher or lower verse number. (GospeLink won't let you select a verse number that doesn't exist.)

NOTE: As you change your selection in Scripture Explorer, the preview window in the lower right corner will display the scripture currently selected.

USING SCRIPTURE SETS

A powerful feature of Scripture Explorer is the Scripture Sets. Scripture Sets identify stories, miracles, and parables that you might want to study or refer to in a talk or lesson. The Sets group these selected scripture passages together so it is easy to find and use what you are looking for. For example, if you are looking for the miracle of parting the Red Sea, you might look in the Scripture Set called "Old Testament: Miracles." If you are looking for the parable of the lost sheep, you might look in the Scripture Set called "New Testament: Parables."

 TO SELECT A SCRIPTURE PASSAGE FROM THE SCRIPTURE SETS:

1. Click the down arrow at the top of the Scripture Sets window to display the different sets.

2. Click the set you are interested in (for example, "Stories: New Testament"). A list of the scripture passages in the Scripture Set you selected will be displayed.

3. Click the name of a scripture passage in the window below the list of sets (for example, "Birth of John the Baptist").

The passage will be displayed in the window on the right, and the reference will appear in the scripture selection boxes on the upper right.

You can go directly to the passage in the Scriptures window by clicking the **Go To** button.

SEARCHING THE SCRIPTURES

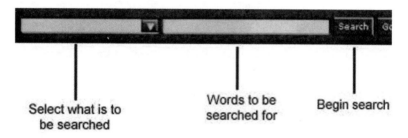

Select what is to be searched

Words to be searched for

Begin search

You can use the Scripture Explorer to search the scriptures. You can even limit your search to a specific volume, such as the New Testament, or a specific book, such as Matthew.

 TO SEARCH ALL THE SCRIPTURES:

1. Click the down arrow on the box at the bottom left of Scripture Explorer.

2. Click **Search all the Scriptures.**

3. In the box on the right, type the word, words, or phrase you want to search for. (Enclose a phrase in quotation marks, "like this.")

4. Click the **Search** button.

The results of your search will be displayed in the Scriptures window.

 TO SEARCH A SPECIFIC VOLUME OF SCRIPTURE:

1. Click one of the volume buttons at the top of Scripture Explorer: **Old Testament, New Testament, Book of Mormon, Doctrine and Covenants,** or **Pearl of Great Price.**

2. Click the down arrow on the box at the bottom left.

3. Click **Search selected volume.**

4. In the box on the right, type the word, words, or phrase you want to search for. (Enclose a phrase in quotation marks, "like this.")

5. Click the **Search** button.

The results of your search will be displayed in the Scriptures window.

 TO SEARCH A SPECIFIC BOOK OF SCRIPTURE:

1. Click one of the volume buttons at the top of Scripture Explorer: **Old Testament, New Testament, Book of Mormon, Doctrine and Covenants,** or **Pearl of Great Price.**

2. Click the name of the book you want to search in the **Select a book** window.

3. Click the down arrow on the box at the bottom left.

4. Click **Search selected book.**

5. In the box on the right, type the word, words, or phrase you want to search for. (Enclose a phrase in quotation marks, "like this.")

6. Click the **Search** button.

The results of your search will be displayed in the Scriptures window.

NOTE: If the word, words, or phrase you searched for does not appear in the book, volume, or entire set of scriptures you are searching, GospeLink Explorer will return you to the main GospeLink window.

CHAPTER 13
TOPIC EXPLORER

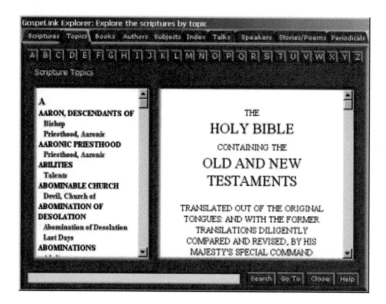

Topic Explorer works like the Topical Guide in your scriptures. In fact, it's an electronic version of *A Topical Guide to the Scriptures,* published by Deseret Book in 1977. The fact that it's electronic means you can link directly to references and perform other useful tasks. You can select a topic in the left window and see the related scripture references in the right window. Then you can go to one of those references in the Scriptures window. You can also search for a topic.

 TO START TOPIC EXPLORER:

1. Click the **Explorer** button on the main toolbar.
2. Click the **Topics** tab.

USING THE TOPIC EXPLORER ALPHABET BAR

A B C D E F G H I J K L M

Use the alphabet bar at the top of Topic Explorer to quickly find the topic you are looking for. Each button displays the topics that start with that letter in the Scripture Topics window. For example:

A	Displays the topics that begin with A.
B	Displays the topics that begin with B.
C	Displays the topics that begin with C.

and so on.

 TO USE THE ALPHABET BAR:

1. Click an alphabet button to display the list of topics that begin with that letter.

2. Click a topic you are interested in.

SEARCHING TOPICS

You can also use Topic Explorer to search for topics. It is designed to search a predetermined list of topics, created from Deseret Book's *A Topical Guide to the Scriptures*. It is not designed to search for text in the library.

 TO SEARCH FOR A TOPIC:

1. Enter a word, words, or phrase in the Search box at the bottom of the window. (Enclose a phrase in quotation marks, "like this.")

2. Click the **Search** button.

If your search found the topic you were looking for, it will be highlighted in the Scripture Topics window on the left. When you click on the highlighted words, related scripture references will appear in the window on the right. For example, if you search for the words *new and everlasting covenant*, the words will be highlighted in the Scripture Topics window on the left. If you click on the highlighted words, the window on the right will display scriptures relating to the new and everlasting covenant.

CHAPTER 14

BOOK EXPLORER

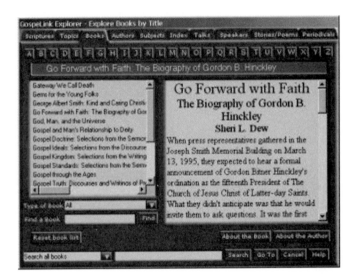

Book Explorer is like the title section of a library's card catalog, only smarter. You can use Book Explorer to find books by title. With Book Explorer you can also:

- Select certain types of books to view, such as biographies, histories, commentaries, and so on.
- Search for a title based on words in that title.
- Search the text of a specific book or of all the books in the library.
- Learn more about a book and its author.

 TO START BOOK EXPLORER:

1. Click the **Explorer** button on the main toolbar.
2. Click the **Books** tab.

USING BOOK EXPLORER'S ALPHABET BAR

Use the alphabet bar at the top of Book Explorer to quickly find the book you are looking for. Each button displays the titles of books that start with that letter. For example:

A	Displays the titles that begin with A.
B	Displays the titles that begin with B.
C	Displays the titles that begin with C.

and so on.

 TO USE THE ALPHABET BAR:

1. Click an alphabet button to display the list of books that begin with that letter.

2. Click a book you are interested in.

USING THE BOOK LIST

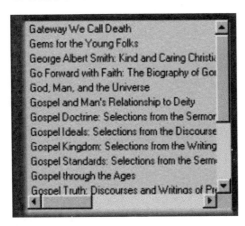

Book Explorer displays lists of all the books in GospeLink. You can use these lists to select a book you are looking for.

TO SELECT A BOOK:

1. Use the alphabet bar and the scroll bar to find the book you are looking for.

2. Click the book with the mouse.

The selected book will be highlighted, and its title will appear in the title label at the top of the screen. Where available, information about the book will appear in the preview window on the right.

3. Double-click the book to go to it in the Books window.

FINDING A BOOK

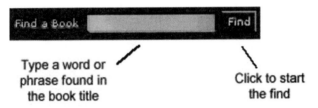

Type a word or phrase found in the book title

Click to start the find

If you're having trouble finding the title of a book you need, you can use the **Find a Book** box in Book Explorer to search for words in the book's title.

 TO USE THE FIND A BOOK WINDOW:

1. Type a word from the title of the book you are looking for in the **Find a Book** box.

2. Click the **Find** button.

The book list will display the titles containing the word you are looking for. For example, if you type in the word *love* and click the **Find** button, the book list will display in alphabetical order all the titles containing the word *love,* starting with *Best-Loved Poems of the LDS People.*

NOTE: If you're looking for more than one word, the words must appear *together* in the title. Otherwise, the title won't be found. For example, if you're looking for *Go Forward with Faith* and search for *Forward* and *Faith* at the same time, you won't find anything. If you search for *Forward with Faith,* however, you'll find the book you're looking for. If you think you know the words in a title but are having trouble finding it, you might try searching for only one of the words. If your search is unsuccessful, try a different word.

SELECTING A TYPE OF BOOK

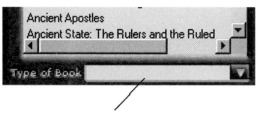

Click down arrow to see Type of Book list

Book Explorer lets you select the type of book you want to see. For example, you can list biographies or doctrinal books or scripture commentaries. The titles of books in these categories will be displayed in the book list.

 TO SELECT A TYPE OF BOOK:

1. Click the down arrow on the right of the **Type of Book** box.
2. Scroll through the list until you see the type of book you are interested in.
3. Click on the type of book to display books in that category in the book list.

TYPES OF BOOKS

Book Explorer categorizes books as the following types:
- Apologetics (books defending the Church)
- Art, Photography, Poetry, Music
- Biography
- Christmas
- Doctrinal
- Essays, Talks
- Gospel Living
- Historical
- LDS Classics
- Marriage and Family
- Missionary
- Patriotic
- Reference
- Scholarly
- Scripture Commentaries
- Self-help, Inspirational

- Teachings of the Prophets
- Women's Interests
- Youth

RESETTING THE BOOK LIST

After you've been working in Book Explorer for a while, you may want to reset the book list to the way it originally appeared. To do so, click the **Reset book list** button at the bottom left of the Book Explorer window:

The **Reset book list** button will redisplay the books alphabetically by title.

LEARNING ABOUT BOOKS AND AUTHORS

Use Book Explorer to learn more about a book and its author. This information is displayed in the information window on the bottom right side of the screen. Often, this information comes directly from the book's jacket, but sometimes it has been written especially for GospeLink.

About the Book	Displays information about the book.
About the Author	Displays information about the author.

You may need to use the scroll bar to see all the information.

SEARCHING FROM BOOK EXPLORER

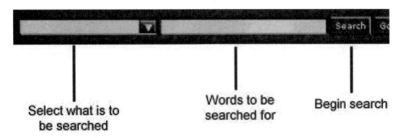

Select what is to be searched
Words to be searched for
Begin search

You can use Book Explorer to search the text of books in the library. You can even limit your search to a specific book, such as *Christ and the New Covenant.*

 TO SEARCH ALL THE BOOKS:

1. Click the down arrow on the box at the bottom left.

2. Click **Search all books.**

3. In the box on the right, type the word, words, or phrase you want to search for. (Enclose a phrase in quotation marks, "like this.")

4. Click the **Search** button.

The results of your search will be displayed in the Books window. For example, if you search all books for the phrase *without guile,* the Books window will display a list of all books in GospeLink containing that phrase, as well as the text of those books with the phrase highlighted.

 TO SEARCH A SPECIFIC BOOK:

1. Click the title of a book in the book list on the left of Book Explorer. The title will be displayed in the selection label above the book list.

2. Click the down arrow on the box at the bottom left.

3. Click **Search selected book.**

4. In the box on the right, type the word, words, or phrase you want to search for. (Enclose a phrase in quotation marks, "like this.")

5. Click the **Search** button.

The results of your search will be displayed in the Books window. For example, if you select the book *Understanding Paul* by Richard

Lloyd Anderson, and then search for the word *charity* in that specific book, the Books window will display a list of pages in that book containing the word *charity*, as well as the text of the book with the word highlighted.

CHAPTER 15
AUTHOR EXPLORER

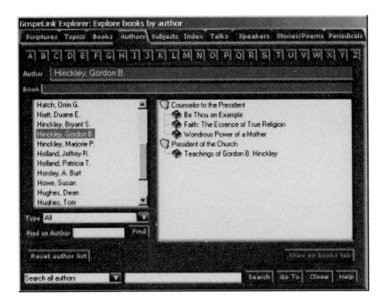

Author Explorer is like the author section of a library's card catalog, only smarter. You can use Author Explorer to find books by author. With Author Explorer you can also:

- Select certain types of authors, such as Church presidents, counselors, apostles, and so on.
- Search for an author.
- Search the text of books by written a certain author or by all of the authors.

 TO START AUTHOR EXPLORER:

1. Click the **Explorer** button on the main toolbar.
2. Click the **Author** tab.

USING AUTHOR EXPLORER'S ALPHABET BAR

Use the alphabet bar at the top of Author Explorer to quickly find the book you are looking for. Each button displays the names of authors whose last name starts with that letter. For example:

A	Displays the names that begin with A.
B	Displays the names that begin with B.
C	Displays the names that begin with C.

and so on.

 TO USE THE ALPHABET BAR:

1. Click an alphabet button to display the list of author names that begin with that letter.

2. Click an author you are interested in.

USING THE AUTHOR LIST

Author Explorer displays a list of the authors whose books are in GospeLink. You can use this list to select an author you are looking for.

 TO SELECT AN AUTHOR:

1. Use the alphabet bar and the scroll bar to find the author you are looking for.

2. Click the author's name with the mouse.

The selected author will be highlighted, and the author's name will appear in the **Author** label at the top of the screen.

FINDING AN AUTHOR

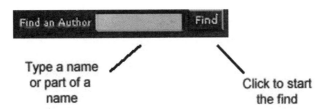

If you're having trouble finding the author of a book you need, you can use the **Find an Author** box to search for the author's name. Or you can use this box if you know the author's name and want to go to it quickly without scrolling the list.

 TO USE THE FIND AN AUTHOR WINDOW:

1. Type a name or part of a name in the **Find an Author** box.
2. Click the **Find** button.

The author list will display the authors matching the names you're looking for. For example, if you search for the name *Smith*, you'll find the names of Joseph Smith, Joseph Fielding Smith, Lucy Mack Smith, and so on.

NOTE: Authors are listed last name first. Also, if you type in two or more parts of a name, those parts must appear *together* in the name. Otherwise, the name won't be found. For example, if you search for *Joseph Fielding Smith*, you won't find anything. Similarly, if you search for *Smith, Fielding*, you won't find anything. But if you search for *Smith, Joseph*, you'll find *Smith, Joseph; Smith, Joseph Fielding; Smith, Joseph F.;* and so on.

SELECTING A TYPE OF AUTHOR

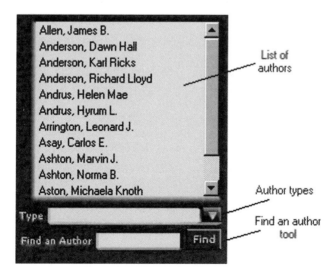

List of authors

Author types

Find an author tool

Author Explorer lets you select the type of author you want to see. For example, you can list Church presidents, counselors, apostles, and so on. The names of authors that fit this description will be displayed in the author list.

 TO SELECT A TYPE OF AUTHOR:
1. Click the down arrow on the right of the **Type** box.
2. Scroll through the list until you see the type of author you want.
3. Click on the type of author you want to see.

TYPES OF AUTHORS
Author Explorer categorizes authors as the following types:
- Apostle
- Church Member
- Counselor to the President
- Non-LDS Author
- Other General Authority
- President of the Church
- Various General Authorities (used with compilations)

RESETTING THE AUTHOR LIST

After you've been working in Author Explorer for a while, you may want to reset the author list to the way it originally appeared. To do so, click the **Reset author list** button:

The **Reset author list** button will redisplay the authors alphabetically by last name.

USING THE LIST OF BOOKS

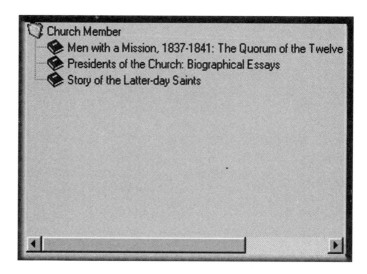

The window on the right of Author Explorer displays the books of the author selected in the author list on the left. The list is in outline form, with the books grouped by the author's position at the time they were written. For example, if you select Joseph Fielding Smith, you'll see the books he wrote as Apostle, Church Member, Counselor to the President, and President of the Church.

Each position is represented by a folder icon, like this:

You can click these folders to view or hide the books they contain.

Each book is represented by a book icon, like this:

You can click a book to select it. Then you can display the book on the Books tab or go to it in the Books window.

SHOWING BOOKS IN BOOK EXPLORER

Once you've selected a book with Author Explorer, you can learn more about it and use it in other ways by displaying it in Book Explorer. To do so, click the **Show on books tab** button:

Show on books tab

The Book Explorer will open with the book displayed.

NOTE: To return to Author Explorer, click the **Authors** tab at the top of the window.

SEARCHING FROM AUTHOR EXPLORER

Select what is to be searched | Words to be searched for | Begin search

You can use Author Explorer to search the text of books in the library. You can limit your search to books by a specific author, such as those by Gordon B. Hinckley, or even to a specific book.

 TO SEARCH BOOKS BY ALL AUTHORS:

1. Click the down arrow on the box at the bottom left of Author Explorer.

2. Click **Search all authors.**

3. In the box on the right, type the word, words, or phrase you want to search for. (Enclose a phrase in quotation marks, "like this.")

4. Click the **Search** button.

The results of your search will be displayed in the Books window.

TO SEARCH BOOKS BY A SPECIFIC AUTHOR:

1. Click the name of an author in the author list on the left of Author Explorer. The author's name will be displayed in the selection label above the book list.

2. Click the down arrow on the box at the bottom left of Author Explorer.

3. Click **Search selected author.**

4. In the box on the right, type the word, words, or phrase you want to search for. (Enclose a phrase in quotation marks, "like this.")

5. Click the **Search** button.

The results of your search will be displayed in the Books window.

Search selected author	Searches only books by the selected author. If you select Neal A. Maxwell, for example, only books by Elder Maxwell will be searched.
Search all authors	Searches all the books in the library.

CHAPTER 16
SUBJECT EXPLORER

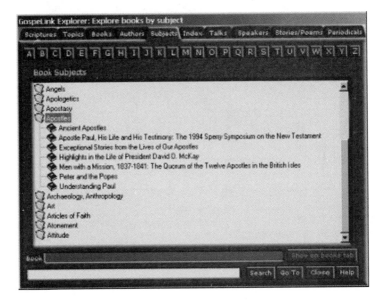

Subject Explorer is like the subject section of a library's card catalog, only smarter. You can use Subject Explorer to find books by subject. You can select certain subjects to look under, such as accountability, adversity, and so on. You can also search the text of a book you have selected.

 TO START SUBJECT EXPLORER:

1. Click the **Explorer** button on the main toolbar.
2. Click the **Subjects** tab.

USING SUBJECT EXPLORER'S ALPHABET BAR

Use the alphabet bar at the top of Subject Explorer to quickly find the book you are looking for. Each button displays the names of subjects that start with that letter. For example:

A	Displays the subjects that begin with A.
B	Displays the subjects that begin with B.
C	Displays the subjects that begin with C.

and so on.

 TO USE THE ALPHABET BAR:

1. Click an alphabet button to display the list of subjects that begin with that letter.

2. Click a subject you are interested in.

USING THE LIST OF SUBJECTS

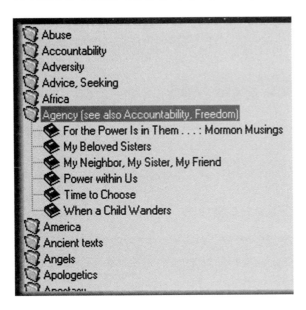

The Book Subjects window in Subject Explorer displays a list of books organized by subject, such as accountability, adversity, and so on.

Each subject is represented by a folder icon, like this:

You can click these folders to view or hide the books they contain.

Each book is represented by a book icon, like this:

You can click a book to select it. Then you can display the book on the Books tab or go to it in the Books window.

SHOWING BOOKS IN BOOK EXPLORER

Once you've selected a book with Subject Explorer, you can learn more about it and use it in other ways by displaying it in Book Explorer. To do so, click the **Show on books tab** button:

Show on books tab

The Book Explorer will open with the book displayed.

NOTE: To return to Subject Explorer, click the **Subjects** tab.

SEARCHING FROM SUBJECT EXPLORER

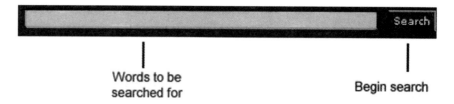

Words to be
searched for

Begin search

After you have selected a book on a certain topic, you can use Subject Explorer to search the text of that book.

 TO SEARCH A SELECTED BOOK:

    1. Select a book in the **Book Subjects** window. The name of the book will appear in the selection label under the window.

    2. In the box below the selection label, type the word, words, or phrase you want to search for. (Enclose a phrase in quotation marks, "like this.")

    3. Click the **Search** button.

The results of your search will be displayed in the Books window.

CHAPTER 17

INDEX EXPLORER

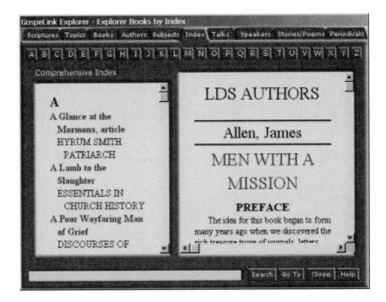

Index Explorer displays GospeLink's Comprehensive Index, which includes the indexes from the LDS books in the library. You can use Index Explorer to find information by index entry. You can also use it to look up literally thousands of topics. Then you can preview or go to the passages that discuss one of those topics.

The Comprehensive Index is important because:

- It lets you find specific information *without* doing a search, so you don't have to wade through hundreds of meaningless search matches, or "hits."

- It lets you find passages about a topic such as faith, even if the word *faith* is never mentioned. Such passages would be extremely difficult to find with a keyword search.

- It identifies book passages that professional indexers over many decades have considered important enough to include in an index. In other words, it identifies not just the location of passages but of the passages that are *worth* locating.

- It identifies thousands of topics and variations on those topics that you might never think of while doing a search. These greatly expand your ability to pinpoint the information you need.
- It lets you quickly see what a variety of authors have to say about a certain topic.

NOTE: If you didn't install the complete Comprehensive Index, you can still do so by following the instructions on page 140.

 TO START INDEX EXPLORER:
1. Click the **Explorer** button on the main toolbar.
2. Click the **Index** tab.

USING INDEX EXPLORER'S ALPHABET BAR

You can use the alphabet bar at the top of Index Explorer to find the index entries you're looking for. Each button displays entries that start with that letter. For example:

A	Displays entries that begin with A.
B	Displays entries that begin with B.
C	Displays entries that begin with C.

and so on.

 TO USE THE ALPHABET BAR:
1. Click an alphabet button to display the list of entries that begin with that letter.
2. Click a topic you are interested in.
The index entries will be displayed in maroon text in the window on the left, with the books they refer to listed underneath them in blue.

Using the List of Index Entries

1. Find an entry by using the alphabet bar and the scroll bar. A list of titles will appear under the entry in blue.

2. Click the title of the book you're interested in. The passage from the book will be displayed in the window on the right.

You can preview the passage in Index Explorer, or you can click the **Go To** button to jump to the passage in the Books window.

For example, if you go to the index entry **Marriage,** a list of books with pertinent passages on marriage will appear under that entry, beginning with *Answers to Gospel Questions, Vol. 4.* You can scroll the list until you find a book you are interested in. Then you can preview the passage in Index Explorer or go to it in the Books window.

TIP: Index Explorer finds the pages on which a topic is discussed, not the topic itself. In other words, it works differently from a search: It doesn't find matches to a word; it finds entire passages that discuss a topic. If you're used to seeing highlighted matches or "hits," this may seem confusing at first because nothing in the passage will be highlighted, and you may have to scroll up or down a little to find the exact information you need. This is exactly the way an index works in a printed book: You look up a topic, turn to the specified page, and then look through the page to find the information. Although this is not as exact as a word search, it's often more efficient because you avoid looking through all of the matches that have no bearing on what you're looking for. After you've tried using the Comprehensive Index a few times, we think you'll like it a lot.

Searching Index Entries

You can also search for index entries in the Comprehensive Index. Index Explorer searches the Comprehensive Index itself, not the text in the library. Once you find an entry you are interested in, you can preview book passages about that entry, or you can click the **Go To** button to go to the passage in the Books window.

 To search for an index entry:

1. Enter a word, words, or a phrase in the box at the bottom of the window. (Enclose a phrase in quotation marks, "like this.")

2. Click the **Search** button.

If your search was successful, you'll see the matches highlighted in the index entries in the left window.

TO MOVE TO THE NEXT MATCH:

1. Click the left index window with the right mouse button. A pop-up menu will appear.
2. Click **Next match.**

TO MOVE TO THE PREVIOUS MATCH:

1. Click the left index window with the right mouse button. A pop-up menu will appear.
2. Click **Previous match.**

For example, if you search for the word *marriage* in the Search box at the bottom of Index Explorer, all index entries containing the word *marriage* will appear, beginning with **Aaron, Complains of Moses' Marriage.** Each entry will be followed by a book or books that you can preview in Index Explorer or go to in the Books window.

INSTALLING OR DELETING THE COMPREHENSIVE INDEX

When you installed GospeLink, you had the option of installing the complete Comprehensive Index on your hard drive or using a smaller version of the index when using Disk A. If you didn't install the complete index on your hard drive, you can still do so by copying it from the Installation Disk.

TO COPY THE COMPREHENSIVE INDEX TO YOUR HARD DRIVE:

1. Put the Installation Disk into your CD-ROM drive.
2. Use Windows Explorer to open the **nfo** directory on the Installation Disk.
3. Copy the file named **compindx.nfo.**
4. Paste the file into your GospeLink directory on your hard drive. Your GospeLink directory probably resides at **C:\Program Files\GospeLink.**

To remove the Comprehensive Index from your hard drive:

1. Use Windows Explorer to open the GospeLink directory on your hard drive. Your GospeLink directory probably resides at **C:\Program Files\GospeLink.**

2. Delete the file named **compindx.nfo.**

NOTE: If you remove the Comprehensive Index from your hard drive, you will still be able to use the smaller, more limited version of the index when using Disk A.

CHAPTER 18
TALK EXPLORER

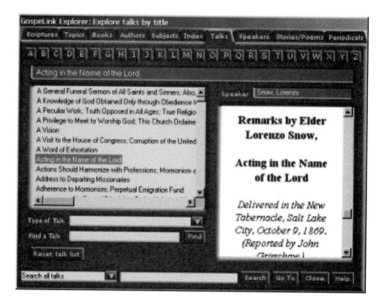

You can use Talk Explorer to find talks in a variety of ways. For example, you can

- Browse talks by title.
- See talks by topic, such as faith or service.
- Search for a talk's title based on words in that title.
- Search the text of a talk or all the talks.

NOTE: Use Talk Explorer to find talks in Conference Reports and *Journal of Discourses*, which are available when using Disk B.

TIP: To find a talk by speaker, use the Speaker Explorer tab in GospeLink Explorer.

 TO START TALK EXPLORER:

1. Click the **Explorer** button on the main toolbar.
2. Click the **Talks** tab.

USING TALK EXPLORER'S ALPHABET BAR

Use the alphabet bar at the top of Talk Explorer to quickly find the talk you are looking for. Each button displays the titles of talks that start with that letter. For example:

A	Displays talks with titles that begin with A.
B	Displays talks with titles that begin with B.
C	Displays talks with titles that begin with C.

and so on.

 TO USE THE ALPHABET BAR:

    1. Click an alphabet button to display the list of talks with titles that begin with that letter.

    2. Click a talk you are interested in.

USING THE LIST OF TALKS

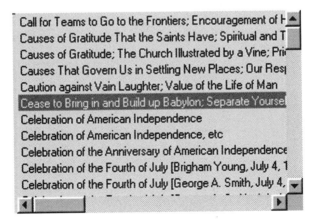

After you select a talk, it will be highlighted, and its title will appear in the title label at the top of the screen. In addition, the speaker's name will appear in the speaker label below the title and to the right. You can preview the talk in the window on the right.

TIP: Some talk titles are long, especially those in the *Journal of Discourses*. If a title isn't completely visible in the list, you can rest the mouse pointer over it for a second or two. A small box will appear showing more of the title. Some talks have no title and are listed by the name of the speaker and the name of the session of general conference at which the talk was given.

FINDING A TALK

If you're having trouble finding the title of a talk you need, you can use the **Find a Talk** box to search for words in the talk's title.

 TO USE THE FIND A TALK WINDOW:

1. Type a word or phrase you are looking for in the **Find a Talk** box.

2. Click the **Find** button.

The talk list will display the titles containing the word or words you are looking for.

NOTE: If you're looking for more than one word, the words must appear *together* in the title. Otherwise, the title won't be found. For example, if you're looking for A *Word of Exhortation* and search for *Word* and *Exhortation* at the same time, you won't find anything. If you search for *Word of Exhortation*, however, you'll find the talk you're looking for. If you think you know the words in a title but are having trouble finding it, you might try searching for only one of the words. If your search is unsuccessful, try a different word.

SELECTING A TYPE OF TALK

Talk Explorer lets you select the type of talk you want to see based on a topic. For example, you can find talks on accountability, adversity, atonement, and dozens of other topics. The titles of these talks will be displayed in the talk list:

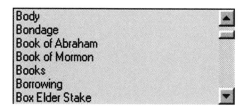

 TO SELECT A TYPE OF TALK:

    1. Click the down arrow on the right of the **Type of Talk** box.

    2. Scroll through the list until you see the topic you are interested in.

    3. Click on the topic to see the list of talks.

RESETTING THE TALK LIST

After you've been working in Talk Explorer for a while, you may want to reset the talk list to the way it originally appeared. To do so, click the **Reset talk list** button:

Reset talk list

The **Reset talk list** button will redisplay the talks alphabetically by title.

SEARCHING FROM TALK EXPLORER

Select what is to be searched

Words to be searched for

Begin search

You can also use Talk Explorer to search the text of talks in the library. You can even limit your search to a specific talk, such as John Taylor's "The Kingdom of God or Nothing."

 TO SEARCH ALL THE TALKS:

1. Click the down arrow on the box at the bottom left.

2. Click **Search all talks.**

3. In the box on the right, type the word, words, or phrase you want to search for. (Enclose a phrase in quotation marks, "like this.")

4. Click the **Search** button.

The results of your search will be displayed in the Books window. For example, if you select **Search all talks** and then type in the phrase *broken heart and contrite spirit,* the Books window will display a list of talks containing those words, as well as the text of those talks with the words highlighted.

 TO SEARCH A SPECIFIC TALK:

1. Click the title of a talk in the talk list on the left of Talk Explorer. (The title will then be displayed in the selection label above the talk list.)

2. Click the down arrow on the box at the bottom left.

3. Click **Search selected talk.**

4. In the box on the right, type the word, words, or phrase you want to search for. (Enclose a phrase in quotation marks, "like this.")

5. Click the **Search** button.

The results of your search will be displayed in the Books window. For example, if you select the talk "Early Events of the Church" by Wilford Woodruff and search for the words *Book of Mormon* in that specific talk, the Books window will display a list of pages in that talk containing the words *Book of Mormon,* as well as the text of the talk with those words highlighted.

NOTE: If your search doesn't find anything, GospeLink Explorer will return you to the main GospeLink window.

CHAPTER 19

SPEAKER EXPLORER

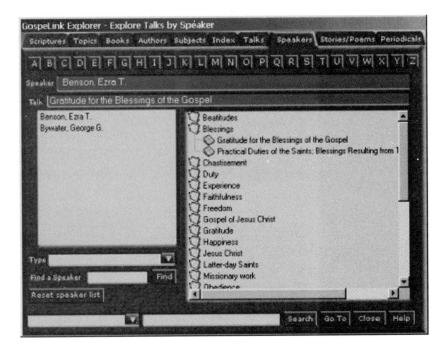

You can use Speaker Explorer to find talks in a variety of ways. For example, you can

- See talks by speaker.
- See talks by topic, such as faith or service.
- Search for a speaker.
- Search the text of a talk or all the talks.

NOTE: Use Speaker Explorer to find talks in Conference Reports and *Journal of Discourses,* which are available when using Disk B.

 TO START SPEAKER EXPLORER:

1. Click the **Explorer** button on the main toolbar.
2. Click the **Speakers** tab.

USING SPEAKER EXPLORER'S ALPHABET BAR

Use the alphabet bar at the top of Speaker Explorer to quickly find the speaker you are looking for. Each button displays the speakers' names that start with that letter. For example:

A	Displays speakers whose last names begin with A.
B	Displays speakers whose last names begin with B.
C	Displays speakers whose last names begin with C.

and so on.

  TO USE THE ALPHABET BAR:

   1. Click an alphabet button to display the list of speaker names that begin with that letter.
   2. Click the speaker's name with the mouse.

Cahoon, Lysle R.
Callis, Charles
Callis, Charles A.
Callis, Charles C.
Cameron, David
Cannon, Angus M.
Cannon, David H.
Cannon, Eugene M.
Cannon, George J.
Cannon, George M.
Cannon, George Q.
Cannon, Hugh J.

The selected speaker will be highlighted, and the speaker's name will appear in the Speaker label at the top of the screen. In addition, topics addressed by that speaker will appear in the window on the right.

FINDING A SPEAKER

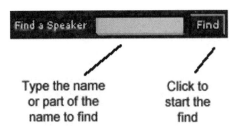

Type the name   Click to
or part of the   start the
name to find   find

If you're having trouble finding a speaker, you can use the **Find a Speaker** box to search for the speaker's name. Or you can use this window if you know the speaker's name and want to go to it quickly without scrolling the list.

 TO USE THE FIND A SPEAKER WINDOW:

1. Type a name or part of a name in the **Find a Speaker** window.
2. Click the **Find** button.

The speaker list will display the speakers matching the names you're looking for. For example, if you search for the name *Smith,* you'll find the names of George Albert Smith, Joseph F. Smith, Joseph Fielding Smith, and so on.

NOTE: Speakers are listed last name first. Also, if you type in two or more parts of a name, those parts must appear *together* in the name. Otherwise, the name won't be found. For example, if you search for *Joseph Fielding Smith,* you won't find anything. Similarly, if you search for *Smith, Fielding,* you won't find anything. But if you search for *Smith, Joseph,* you'll find *Smith, Joseph; Smith, Joseph Fielding; Smith, Joseph F.;* and so on.

SELECTING A TYPE OF SPEAKER

Speaker Explorer lets you select the type of speaker you want to see. For example, you can list Church presidents, counselors, apostles, and so on. The names of speakers that fit this description will be displayed in the speaker list. For example, if you select **Apostle,** the list will look something like this:

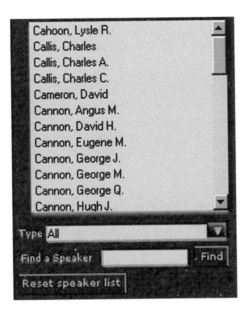

 To SELECT A TYPE OF SPEAKER:

　　1. Click the down arrow on the right of the **Type** box.

　　2. Scroll through the list until you see the type of speaker you're interested in.

　　3. Click on the type of speaker you want to see.

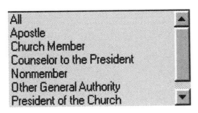

TYPES OF SPEAKERS

Speaker Explorer categorizes speakers as the following types:

- All
- Apostle
- Church Member
- Counselor to the President
- Nonmember
- Other General Authority
- President of the Church
- Various General Authorities (used with compilations)

TIP: GospeLink contains Conference Reports up to 1971. So if you select type of speaker and then select **President of the Church,** you won't see a listing for any Church president from Harold B. Lee on. If you want to find a talk by a President of the Church after 1971—for example, by President Hinckley—the best way to do this is to use the alphabet bar or the Find a Speaker box to search for the speaker by name. You can then see all articles in GospeLink by that speaker. You can also use the Ensign Index button on the main toolbar to find a list of *Ensign* articles by a particular speaker.

RESETTING THE SPEAKER LIST

After you've been working in Speaker Explorer for a while, you may want to reset the speaker list to the way it originally appeared. To do so, click the **Reset speaker list** button.

The list of speakers will be redisplayed alphabetically by last name.

USING THE LIST OF TALKS

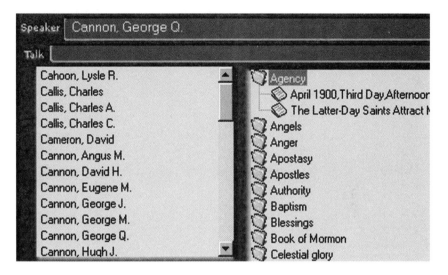

The window on the right of Speaker Explorer displays a list of talks by the speaker selected in the Speaker List on the left. The list is in outline form, with the talks grouped by topic. For example, if you select George Q. Cannon in the Speaker List, you'll see that he gave talks on the topics of agency, angels, anger, apostasy and so on.

Each topic is represented by a folder icon, like this:

You can click these folders to view or hide the talks they contain. Each talk is represented by a talk icon, like this:

You can click a talk to select it. Then you can search the talk or go to it in the Books window.

SEARCHING FROM SPEAKER EXPLORER

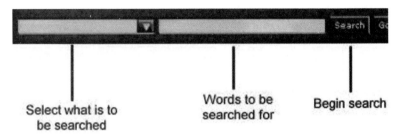

Select what is to
be searched

Words to be
searched for

Begin search

You can use Speaker Explorer to search the text of talks in the library. You can search talks by all speakers or limit your search to a specific talk.

 TO SEARCH TALKS BY ALL SPEAKERS:

1. Click the down arrow on the box at the bottom left.

2. Click **Search all talks.**

3. In the box on the right, type the word, words, or phrase you want to search for. (Enclose a phrase in quotation marks, "like this.")

4. Click the **Search** button.

The results of your search will be displayed in the Books window.

 TO SEARCH A SELECTED TALK:

1. Select a speaker in the Speaker List. (The speaker's name will appear in the display label above the list.)

2. Open a topic folder in the window on the right.

3. Click the name of a talk. (The name will appear in the display label below the name of the speaker.)

4. Click the down arrow on the box at the bottom left.

5. Click **Search selected talk.**

6. In the box on the right, type the word, words, or phrase you want to search for. (Enclose a phrase in quotation marks, "like this.")

7. Click the **Search** button.

The results of your search will be displayed in the Books window.

CHAPTER 20
STORIES/POEMS EXPLORER

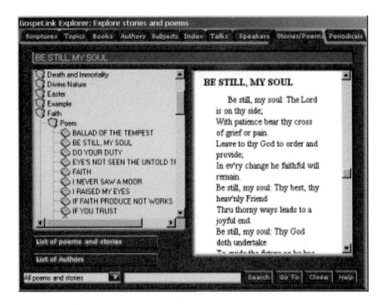

You can use Stories/Poems Explorer to find stories and poems to use in talks and lessons. You can

- See stories and poems by topic.
- See stories and poems by author.
- Search the text of stories and poems.

 TO START STORIES/POEMS EXPLORER:

1. Click the **Explorer** button on the main toolbar.
2. Click the **Stories/Poems** tab.

USING THE LIST OF STORIES AND POEMS

The window on the left of Stories/Poems Explorer displays a list of topics, stories, and poems or a list of authors, stories, and poems, depending on which button you click.

The list is in outline form.

Authors and topics are represented by folder icons, like this:

You can click these folders to view or hide what they contain.

Each story or poem is represented by an icon like this:

You can preview the story or poem it represents in the window on the right. You can also search the story or poem or go to it in the Books window.

TO SHOW THE LIST OF STORIES AND POEMS BY TOPIC:
Click the **List of Stories and Poems** button.

TO SHOW THE LIST OF STORIES AND POEMS BY AUTHOR:
Click the **List of Authors** button.

TO SELECT A STORY OR POEM:
Click the title of the story or poem.

TO PREVIEW A STORY OR POEM:

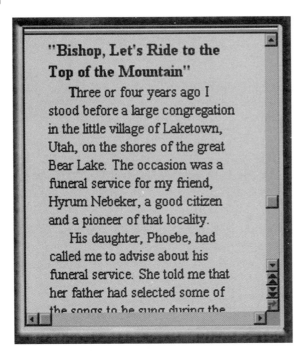

When you select a story or poem, it will be displayed in the window on the right. This will let you decide if the story or poem will fit your needs before you go to it.

TO GO TO THE STORY OR POEM:

1. Click the title of the story or poem.
2. Click the **Go To** button.

The story or poem will be displayed in the Books window.

SEARCHING FROM STORIES/POEMS EXPLORER

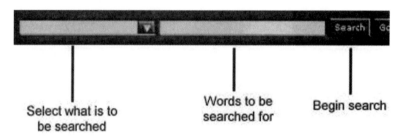

Select what is to be searched

Words to be searched for

Begin search

You can use Stories/Poems Explorer to search the text of stories and poems in the library.

 TO SEARCH ALL STORIES AND POEMS:

1. Click the down arrow on the box at the bottom left.
2. Click **All stories and poems.**
3. In the box on the right, type the word, words, or phrase you want to search for. (Enclose a phrase in quotation marks, "like this.")
4. Click the **Search** button.

The results of your search will be displayed in the Books window.

NOTE: You can also choose to search all stories or all poems.

CHAPTER 21
PERIODICAL EXPLORER

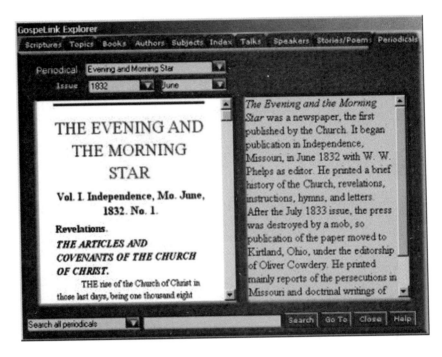

You can use Periodical Explorer to:

- Find articles by periodical and issue.
- Read about the periodicals.
- Search the text of all periodicals, a selected periodical (such as the *Improvement Era*), or a selected issue (such as May 1940).

NOTE: LDS periodicals are available when using Disk B.

TIP: To find talks in Conference Reports or *Journal of Discourses*, use Talk Explorer or Speaker Explorer. You can also look through Conference Reports and *Journal of Discourses* chronologically by expanding the Books window full screen, clicking the **Periodicals** button at the bottom of the window, and using the table of contents on the left of the expanded window.

TO START PERIODICAL EXPLORER:

   1. Click the **Explorer** button on the main toolbar.
   2. Click the **Periodicals** tab.

 TO SELECT A PERIODICAL:

   1. Click the down arrow on the right of the **Periodical** list.
   2. Click the title of a periodical you are interested in.
   3. Click the down arrow on the left **Issue** box to select the year.
   4. Click the down arrow on the right **Issue** box to select the month.

   After you've selected a periodical, you can learn more about it in the information window on the right side of the screen. You may need to use the scroll bar to see all the information.

SEARCHING FROM PERIODICAL EXPLORER

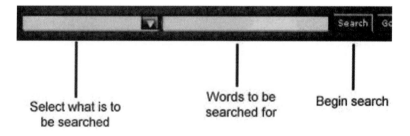

You can use Periodical Explorer to search the text of periodicals in the library, including Conference Reports and *Journal of Discourses*. You can search all periodicals, a specific periodical, or a specific issue.

 TO SEARCH ALL PERIODICALS:

   1. Click the down arrow on the box at the bottom left.
   2. Click **Search all periodicals.**

3. In the box on the right, type the word, words, or phrase you want to search for. (Enclose a phrase in quotation marks, "like this.")

4. Click the **Search** button.

The results of your search will be displayed in the Books window.

 TO SEARCH A SELECTED PERIODICAL:

1. Click the title of a periodical in the list of periodicals.

2. Click the down arrow on the box at the bottom left.

3. Click **Search selected periodical.**

4. In the box on the right, type the word, words, or phrase you want to search for. (Enclose a phrase in quotation marks, "like this.")

5. Click the **Search** button.

The results of your search will be displayed in the Books window.

 TO SEARCH A SELECTED ISSUE:

1. Click the title of a periodical in the list of periodicals.

2. Click the year and month in the **Issue** boxes.

3. Click the down arrow on the box at the bottom left.

4. Click **Search selected issue.**

5. In the box on the right, type the word, words, or phrase you want to search for. (Enclose a phrase in quotation marks, "like this.")

6. Click the **Search** button.

The results of your search will be displayed in the Books window.

CHAPTER 22
ENSIGN INDEX

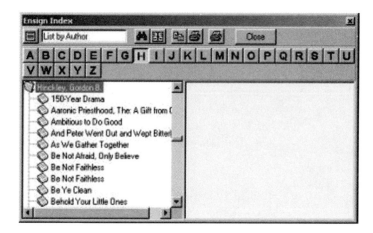

The Ensign Index is a powerful tool you can use to locate articles in the *Ensign* magazine. Whether you have your own collection of the magazines or use those in your ward library, you can save time by using the Ensign Index to find the articles you need and identify the issues and page numbers where they appear. You can find an article by title, author, subject, feature, or a combination of these.

 TO FIND THE LOCATION OF AN ARTICLE:

1. Click the display button on the top left corner of the Ensign Index window. It allows you to choose how the list of articles will appear. You can choose to have articles listed by subject, author, feature, or title, or by a combination of these.

2. Click the way you want the list to appear. Your selection will show in the display label to the right of the button.

3. Scroll the list to find the article you are interested in. (You may have to open folders to get to the actual article titles.)

4. Click on the article title.

The information about the location of the article in the *Ensign* will be displayed in the window on the right. You can copy the information to the Windows Clipboard or to PrePrint.

TIP: If you're doing extensive research, you may want to copy information about several articles to PrePrint. Then you can print them all at once before looking up the articles in the *Ensign*.

NOTE: The actual text of the *Ensign* is not included in GospeLink. It is copyrighted by The Church of Jesus Christ of Latter-day Saints and is not available at this time.

ENSIGN INDEX TOOLBAR

The Ensign Index toolbar will help you use the index features. To use the toolbar, click the buttons with the mouse.

For example, to print information about an article, click the Print button:

The information will be sent to your default printer.

The following table shows the buttons on the toolbar and what they do:

Button	Name	Function
🗏	Display	Lets you choose the way the list of articles is displayed: • Subject • Subject, then Author • Subject, then Feature • Author • Author, then Subject • Author, then Feature • Feature • Feature, then Subject • Feature, then Author • Title
List by Author	Display label	Describes how the list is currently displayed.
🔍	Search for words	Searches for words in the index.
▦	Search in range	Searches for articles in a specific range of dates.
📋	Copy to Clipboard	Copies selected article information to the Windows Clipboard.
🖨	Print	Prints the selected article information.

	Copy to PrePrint	Copies the selected article information to PrePrint.
Close	Close	Closes the Ensign Index.

NOTE: You can use Tooltips to see what each button does.

ENSIGN INDEX ALPHABET BAR

You can use the alphabet bar at the top of the Ensign Index to display titles, authors, features, and topics alphabetically. Click a button to display the items that begin with that letter.

For example, if you select **List by Author** and then click the **H** alphabet button, only the articles with authors whose last names begin with H will appear on the list. If you select **List by Title** and then click the **S** button, only the articles with titles that begin with the letter S will appear.

LISTING A RANGE OF ARTICLES

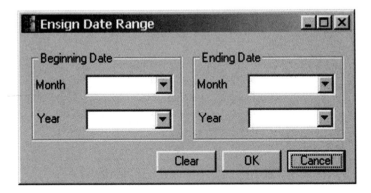

The Ensign Index is so large that sometimes you may want to limit the list of articles to a range of dates. You can see a specific month, a range of years, or anything in between.

TO SEARCH A RANGE OF ARTICLES:

1. Click the **Ensign Index** button on GospeLink's main toolbar.

2. Click the **Set range of dates to search** button.

3. Use the drop-down lists to select beginning and ending dates for months and years.

4. Click **OK** to see the list of articles in the range you have specified. To see all articles, click the **Clear** button.

SEARCHING FOR ARTICLES

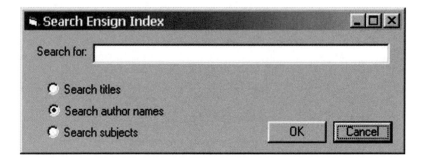

You can search the words in the Ensign Index to find articles by title, author, or subject.

 TO SEARCH THE INDEX:

1. Click the **Search** button on the Ensign Index toolbar.

2. Type the name or word you are searching for in the **Search for** box.

3. Click the category you want to search:
- titles
- author names
- subjects

4. Click **OK.** A list containing the search results will appear in the left window.

SEARCH EXAMPLES

 TO SEARCH FOR WORDS IN A TITLE:

If you wanted to find articles with the word *love* in the title, you would do the following:

1. Type the word *love* in the **Search for** box.

2. Click **Search titles.**

3. Click **OK.**

The list will contain all the article titles that include the word *love.*

If you wanted to find all the articles by authors with the name of *Smith,* you would do the following:

1. Type the name *Smith* in the **Search for** box.

2. Click **Search author names.**

3. Click **OK.**

The list will contain all the authors whose last name is *Smith.*

You can find articles about the subject of faith by searching for the word *faith.*

1. Type the word *faith* in the **Search for** box.

2. Click **Search subjects.**

3. Click **OK.**

The list will contain all the subjects that include the word *faith.*

CHAPTER 23
COMPOSER

Composer is a simple but useful word processor built into GospeLink. It isn't intended to replace your regular word processor, such as Microsoft Word or WordPerfect. Composer will open only one document at a time, and it doesn't include a spell checker. However, it does provide special features you'll find helpful in creating talks and lessons. With Composer you can:

- Copy text directly from GospeLink to Composer without pasting from the Windows Clipboard.
- Copy text from PrePrint to Composer.
- Save from Composer to a PalmPilot file that you can read on your PalmPilot.
- Save text from Composer in an .rtf (rich text format) file that you can open in your regular word processor.

STARTING COMPOSER

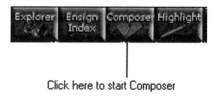

Click here to start Composer

To start Composer, click the **Composer** button on the main toolbar. Composer will also start the first time you copy text to it during a GospeLink session.

USING COMPOSER'S MENUS

FILE

New	Clears Composer and creates a new document. Be sure to save your current document before choosing this option.
Open	Opens a file for you to edit or print.
Save	Saves a file.
Save As	Lets you save a file under a new name.
Send to PalmPilot	Saves to a file you can send to your PalmPilot.
Page Setup	Lets you set the page size, margins, and tabs for your document.
Print Preview	Lets you see how your document will look when printed.
Print	Prints all or selected items.
Print Setup	Lets you set your printer options.
Exit	Closes Composer.

 EDIT

Undo	Undoes the last change you made in Composer.
Cut	Cuts selected text from Composer to the Windows Clipboard.
Copy	Copies selected text from Composer to the Windows Clipboard.
Paste	Pastes text from the Windows Clipboard to Composer.
Clear	Clears all text from the document.

Select All Text	Selects all text in the document.
Find	Finds words or phrases in the document.
Replace	Replaces words or phrases with other words or phrases. Use this feature to find and replace text in your document.

 VIEW

Header and Footer	Lets you see or hide headers and footers. Use headers and footers to repeat information at the top or bottom of every page.

 INSERT

Picture	(Not available.)
Table	Inserts a multi-column table into your document.
Symbol	Inserts a symbol into your document. Symbols include arrows, stars, the copyright mark, and many more.
Date	Inserts the current date into the text.
Time	Inserts the current time into the text.

 FORMAT

Character	Sets the font and color of the selected text or the text for the document.
Paragraph	Sets indentation, spacing, alignment, and tabs for the document.
Bullets and Numbering	Lets you create numbered or bulleted lists.

TABLE

Insert Table	Inserts a multi-column table into your document.
Select Table	Selects the complete table to copy or delete.
Insert Row	Inserts a new row into the table above the current row.
Delete Row	Deletes the current row.
Select Row	Selects the current row.
Insert Cell	Inserts a new cell before the current cell.
Delete Cell	Deletes the current cell.
Merge Cell	Combines the selected cells. **WARNING!** Only the data in the first cell is retained.
Split Cell	Divides a cell into two or more cells.
Cell Height and Width	Changes the selected cell's height and width.
Borders and Shading	Sets the color and shading of the table.
GridLines	Turns gridlines on and off.

 HELP

Contents	Starts the GospeLink Help System.

USING COMPOSER'S TOOLBAR

Button	Name	Function
	New document	Clears Composer and creates a new document. Be sure to save your current document before choosing this option.
	Open	Lets you open a file to edit or print.
	Save	Saves a file.
	Print	Prints all or selected items.
	PrePrint	Lets you see how your document will look when printed.
	Spell check	(Not available.)
	Cut	Cuts selected text from Composer to the Windows Clipboard.
	Copy	Copies selected text from Composer to the Windows Clipboard.
	Paste	Pastes text from the Windows Clipboard to Composer.
	Undo	Undoes the last change you made in Composer.

	Find	Finds words or phrases in the document.
	Table	Inserts a multi-column table into your document.
	Picture	(Not available.)
	Field	(Not available.)
	Date	Inserts the current date into the text.
	Time	Inserts the current time into the text.
	Headers/Footers	Lets you see or hide headers and footers. You can use headers and footers to repeat information at the top or bottom of every page.
	Show all	Reveals codes for paragraphs, markers, and spaces.
Arial	Font	Changes the current font.
12	Point size	Changes the current point size.
	Left justify	Sets paragraph to left justify.
	Center justify	Sets paragraph to center justify.

	Right justify	Sets paragraph to right justify.
	Justify	Sets paragraph to justify.
B	Bold	Formats text as bold.
I	Italic	Formats text as italic.
<u>U</u>	Underline	Formats text as underline.
ABC	Strikeout	Formats text as strikeout.
x^2	Superscript	Formats text as superscript.
x_2	Subscript	Formats text as subscript.
	Single spacing	Formats paragraphing as single space.
	1 1/2 spacing	Formats paragraphing as one and a half space.
	Double spacing	Formats paragraphing as double space.
	Color	Changes the current font color.

CHAPTER 24
HIGHLIGHT

You can use highlighting to mark text you want to remember, just as you would highlight text with a pencil or highlighter in your printed books and scriptures.

 TO CHOOSE A HIGHLIGHTER:

Click the **Highlighter** button on the main toolbar. The following window will be displayed:

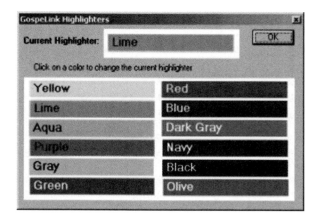

You can select a highlighter by clicking it with the mouse. The highlighter you select will appear in the **Current Highlighter** bar at the top of the window.

 TO HIGHLIGHT TEXT:

You can highlight text in two different ways, as shown in the following table:

Drop-down menu (on each window)	1. Select the text you want to highlight. 2. Click the down arrow for the drop-down menu. 3. Click **Highlight.**

Pop-up menu	1. Select the text you want to highlight. 2. Click the right mouse button. 3. Click **Highlight.**

TIP: If you want to highlight an entire paragraph, you don't have to select it first. All you have to do is click anywhere in the paragraph and then apply the highlighting.

 TO REMOVE HIGHLIGHTING:

You can remove highlighting in two different ways, as shown in the following table:

Drop-down menu (on each window)	1. Select the highlighted text. 2. Click the down arrow for the drop-down menu. 3. Click **Erase Highlight.**
Pop-up menu	1. Select the highlighted text. 2. Click the right mouse button. 3. Click **Erase Highlight.**

TIP: If you want to remove highlighting from an entire paragraph, you don't have to select it first. All you have to do is click anywhere in the paragraph and then remove the highlighting.

NOTE: After you've worked with highlighters, be sure to save your work by clicking on the **Save** button at the top right-hand corner of the screen if you want to retain highlighting.

CHAPTER 25
BOOKMARKS

A powerful feature of GospeLink is the ability to place bookmarks in each of the text windows. Bookmarks are a quick way to get back to information you want to remember.

 TO PLACE A BOOKMARK:

Click in the text where you want to place a bookmark.

Click the down arrow at the top left of the text window. A menu will appear.

Click **Bookmark.**

Type in a name for your bookmark (or use the default name).

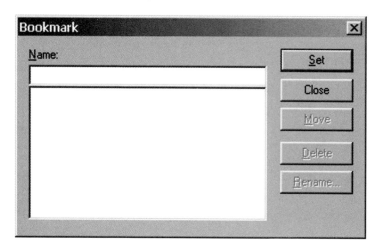

Click **Set.**

 TO FIND A BOOKMARK:

Click the down arrow at the top left of the text window. A menu will appear.

Click **Bookmark.**

Click the bookmark you want to find.

Click **Go To.**

TO MOVE A BOOKMARK:

Click in the text where you want the bookmark to go.

Click the down arrow at the top left of the text window. A menu will appear.

Click **Bookmark.**

Click the bookmark you want to move.

Click **Move.**

 TO DELETE A BOOKMARK:

Click the down arrow at the top left of the text window. A menu will appear.

Click **Bookmark.**

Click the bookmark you want to delete.

Click **Delete.**

Confirm the deletion.

Click **Close.**

 TO RENAME A BOOKMARK:

Click the down arrow at the top left of the text window. A menu will appear.

Click **Bookmark.**

Click the bookmark you want to rename.

Click **Rename.**

Type in the new name.

Click **OK.**

Click **Close.**

CHAPTER 26
PRINTING

All printing in GospeLink is done from PrePrint, which makes printing easy and manageable. To open PrePrint, click the **Printing** button on the main toolbar. The PrePrint window will appear:

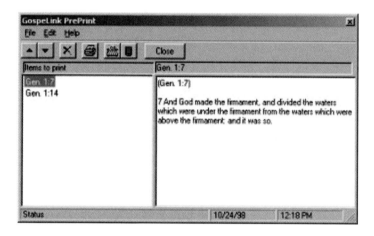

PrePrint stores text items you've previously selected for printing. You can rearrange or delete items in PrePrint and then print all your material at once.

TIP: Use PrePrint as a place to collect all kinds of information that you find as you browse or study. Then you can save it, copy it, or print it.

NOTE: You can resize the PrePrint windows as you would in any Windows application.

PrePrint Toolbar

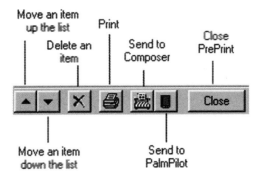

The PrePrint Toolbar lets you quickly use PrePrint's features. To use the toolbar, click the button that performs the feature you want.

For example, to send items to Composer, click the Composer button. The following table lists the PrePrint toolbar buttons and what they do:

Button	Name	Function
▲	Move up	Moves the selected item up the list of items to be printed. PrePrint items will be printed in the order they appear. Items at the top of the list will be printed first.
▼	Move down	Moves the selected item down the list of items to be printed. PrePrint items will be printed in the order they appear. Items at the bottom of the list will be printed last.
✕	Delete	Deletes the selected item from the PrePrint list. Once an item has been deleted it will not be printed.
🖨	Print	Sends the PrePrint items to the default printer.

	Send to Composer	Sends the PrePrint items to Composer.
	Send to PalmPilot	Sends the PrePrint items to your PalmPilot.
Close	Close	Closes PrePrint.

NOTE: Each of the buttons on the toolbar has a Tooltip that will appear if the mouse pointer rests over the button. The Tooltip will remind you what the button does.

PREPRINT MENU

PrePrint includes a standard Windows menu bar above the toolbar. To see the options under each menu item, click that item with your mouse. The drop-down menu will display other options you can choose. The menu bar includes three menus: File, Edit, and Help. The following is a list of the options under each menu item:

FILE

Name	Keyboard option	Function
Save	Alt-F Alt-S	Saves the PrePrint list. If you change the order of the items in the list, be sure to save the new list.
Clear Print	Alt-F Alt-C	Deletes all the items in the PrePrint list. This action cannot be undone.
Print		Sends all items to your printer.
Print Selected Item		Sends a selected item to your printer.
Close	Alt-F Alt-C	Closes PrePrint.

 EDIT

Name	Keyboard option	Function
Delete	Alt-E Alt-D	Deletes a selected item. **WARNING!** This action cannot be undone.
Copy Selected Item		Copies a selected item to the Windows Clipboard.
Copy All		Copies all items to the Windows Clipboard.

HELP

Name	Keyboard option	Function
Contents	Alt-H Alt-C F1	Starts the GospeLink Help System.

PrePrint List

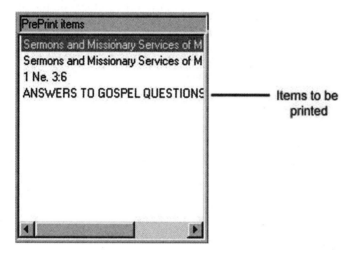

Items to be printed

The PrePrint list displays all the items copied from GospeLink to be printed. The items may include scriptures, excerpts from books, excerpts from periodicals, excerpts from reference works, *Ensign* sources, or personal notes. The items are listed in the order they are copied and will be printed from top to bottom.

The PrePrint list lets you reorder the items you want to print. If you decide to print an item first, you can move it to the top of the list. You can also delete items or add different items to your list.

 TO REORDER ITEMS:

To reorder items in the PrePrint list, do the following:

1. Click an item you want to move. It will be highlighted in a different color.

2. Click the appropriate toolbar button to move the item up or down the list.

▲	Moves the item up the list.
▼	Moves the item down the list.

 TO DELETE ITEMS:

To delete an item from the PrePrint list, do the following:

1. Click the item you want to delete. The item selected will be highlighted in a different color.

2. Click the **Delete** button on the toolbar or the **Delete** option in the **Edit** menu. The item will be deleted.

✕	Deletes the selected item.

WARNING! Be careful not to delete the wrong item. Once it's gone, you can't get it back without finding it again in the GospeLink library and again copying it to PrePrint.

 SAVE

The **Save** menu option lets you save any changes to your PrePrint list. Periodically saving changes is a good idea even though you will be prompted to save the list when you close PrePrint.

 CLEAR PREPRINT

The **Clear PrePrint** option clears all the items from your PrePrint list. You probably won't use this option very often.

PrePrint Viewer

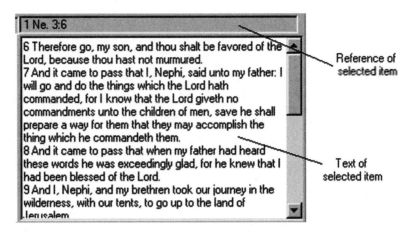

The PrePrint viewer displays the text of a selected item in the PrePrint list. You can select an item by clicking it with your mouse. The item will be highlighted in a different color, and the text will be displayed in the viewer.

NOTE: You cannot edit the text displayed in the viewer. If you want to edit the text, copy it to Composer. You can also copy the text to the Windows Clipboard and paste it into your regular word processor.

Printing from PrePrint

You can print all the items in the PrePrint list or just selected items.

 TO PRINT ALL ITEMS:

Click the **Print** button on the PrePrint toolbar. The items in the PrePrint list will be printed in the order in which they appear.

TO PRINT SELECTED ITEMS:
    1. Click the **File** menu
    2. Click **Print.** The **Print** dialog box will appear. You can print all items or just a selected item.

SENDING TO COMPOSER

Click the **Composer** button on the toolbar to copy the text of all the items in your PrePrint list to Composer. Then you can use Composer to edit the text and add text of your own.

SENDING TO PALMPILOT

Click the **PalmPilot** button on the PrePrint toolbar to copy all the items in your PrePrint list to a document that you can copy to your PalmPilot.

    A dialog box will appear, allowing you to name the document:

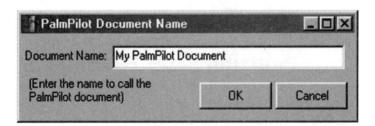

The name you give the document will appear on your PalmPilot, so it should reflect the contents of what is being copied.

    GospeLink will then display a standard Windows save dialog box so you can name the file and specify its location. Then you can download the file to your PalmPilot.

NOTE: You'll need to install the AportisDoc Reader on your PalmPilot in order to copy files to your PalmPilot. (You can also use other PalmPilot doc readers.) For instructions on how to do this, see the **readme** file in the **Palm** folder on your Installation Disk. Also, see your PalmPilot documentation for instructions on downloading files to your PalmPilot.

CLOSING PREPRINT

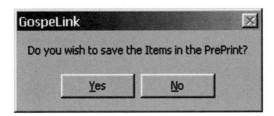

When you close PrePrint, the program will ask if you want to save the items in it. Usually after printing, you'll click **No.** Then PrePrint will be empty the next time you want to use it. If you click **Yes,** the items will remain in PrePrint and be available the next time you open it.

NOTE: If you save the items, they will remain in PrePrint. If you select more items to be printed, they will be added to the end of the list. If you are through with the items, the best thing to do is remove them.

Yes	Click **Yes** to save all the items in PrePrint. If you save them, they will remain in PrePrint, and new items will be added to them.
No	Click **No** to remove all items from PrePrint. The next time you use PrePrint, they will be gone.

CHAPTER 27

OPTIONS

When you click the **Options** button on the GospeLink toolbar, a menu will appear giving you three options:

Set layout options	Changes the display in the main window to one of the following: • **Multiple Windows:** Displays the default three-window view. • **Scriptures Window Only:** Displays the Scriptures window full screen. • **Books Window Only:** Displays the Books window full screen. • **References Window Only:** Displays the References window full screen.
Skip start-up animation	Skips the animation and music when you start GospeLink.
Skip start-up screen	Skips GospeLink's initial sign-on and menu screen.

CHAPTER 28
TOOLS

Switch Disks
Switch to a Different User
Set Zoom to Normal
Start Search Sets Manager
Start Over

When you click the **Tools** button on the GospeLink toolbar, a menu will appear giving you several options:

Switch Disks	Lets you switch the library disks.
Switch to a Different User	Returns to GospeLink's start-up screen, where you can sign on as a different user.
Set Zoom to Normal	Returns text in all windows to the default size.
Start Search Sets Manager	Starts the Search Sets Manager in the Search window.
Start Over	Returns all windows to their starting point.

CHAPTER 29

HELP

GOSPELINK HELP SYSTEM

GospeLink includes a detailed online help system. You can use it through a contents listing, by looking up an item in the index, or by searching for an item you want to learn more about.

TIP: If you're connected to the Internet, you can click on Internet addresses in the help system to take you to different sites.

CONTENTS

You can browse the contents listing of the GospeLink Help System to find the items you want to learn about. To do this:

1. Click the **Help** button on the main toolbar.
2. Click **GospeLink Help System.**
3. Click the **Contents** tab.
4. Double-click the closed book icons to expand them.
5. Double-click the open book icons to compress them.
6. Click on an item you are interested in learning about.
7. Read the Help instructions in the window on the right.

INDEX

The GospeLink Help System includes a thorough index to help you find the items you want to learn about. To use it:

1. Click the **Help** button on the main toolbar.
2. Click **GospeLink Help System.**
3. Click the **Index** tab.
4. Double-click an item you are interested in learning about.
5. Read the Help instructions in the window on the right.

SEARCH

You can search the text of the GospeLink Help System to find the items you want to learn about. To do so:

1. Click the **Help** button on the main toolbar.
2. Click **GospeLink Help System.**
3. Click the **Search** tab.

4. Type the word you want to find into the keyword box on the top left.

5. Click the **List Topics** button.

6. Double-click the topic you are interested in learning about.

7. Read the Help instructions in the window on the right.

TUTORIAL

As part of the help system, an animated tutorial is included with GospeLink. To start the tutorial:

1. Insert the Installation Disk.

2. Click **Run Tutorial.**

3. Click the items you want to learn about.

NOTE: If your computer has a sound card and speakers, you can listen to the tutorial instructions while watching the tutorial on your screen.

You can also use a text-only version of the tutorial. To do so:

1. Click the **Help** button on the main toolbar.

2. Click **Tutorial.**

3. Click the **Contents** tab.

4. Double-click the closed book icons to expand them.

5. Double-click the open book icons to compress them.

6. Click on an item you are interested in learning about.

7. Read the instructions in the window on the right.

QUICK REFERENCE

A quick reference card is included in your GospeLink CD-ROM case. It describes GospeLink's basic features and how to use them. You can also see this information in the program itself. To do so:

1. Click the **Help** button on the main toolbar.

2. Click the **Contents** tab.

3. Click **Quick Reference.**

4. Double-click the closed book icons to expand them.

5. Double-click the open book icons to compress them.

6. Click on an item you are interested in learning about.

7. Read the instructions in the window on the right.

ABOUT

You can go to the About window by clicking the **Help** button on GospeLink's main toolbar and selecting **About**. The About window contains important information about your GospeLink program, including your serial number, which you may be asked to refer to if you call technical support.

TECHNICAL SUPPORT

You can contact GospeLink technical support by calling toll free:
1–877–LDS–LINK (1–877–537–5465)
Be sure to have the following information available:

- The serial number from the back of your CD case.
- The version of Microsoft Windows you are using (95 or 98).
- The screen resolution your computer is set to.
- The amount of memory (RAM) in your computer.
- The amount of free hard-drive space on your computer.

You can also e-mail a description of your problem, with the information listed above, to support@gospelink.com.

CHAPTER 30
SAVE

If you personalize GospeLink by adding bookmarks, highlighters, text notes, or personal notes, and you want to retain this personalization in future sessions of GospeLink, you'll want to save your work by clicking the **Save** button on the main toolbar. This will save all your personalized items for future use. Other users can have their own personalized items.

If you haven't saved your changes when you close GospeLink, you'll be prompted to save at that time. If you choose not to save, all your personalized changes will be lost.

CHAPTER 31
EXIT

To close GospeLink, click the **Exit** button on the main toolbar. If you have made any changes or additions, including bookmarks, highlighters, and personal notes, you will be prompted to save your work. If you choose not to save, all your changes will be lost.

NOTE: Be sure to save your work if you want to retain your personalization of GospeLink!

PART 4: USING GOSPELINK WITH YOUR PALMPILOT

CHAPTER 32
PALMPILOT

If you own a PalmPilot, the "personal digital assistant" from 3Com, you can select text from GospeLink and send it to your PalmPilot. This is useful for all kinds of things—everything from studying on the road to going over notes for a talk. To send text from GospeLink to your PalmPilot, you'll need to install the AportisDoc Reader on your PalmPilot. (You can also use other PalmPilot doc readers.) As an introductory offer, the AportisDoc Reader is included free with GospeLink. For instructions on how to install it, see the **readme** file in the **Palm** folder on your Installation Disk. Also, be sure to read the other documentation in that folder. In addition, see your PalmPilot documentation for instructions on downloading files to your PalmPilot.

COPYING TO YOUR PALMPILOT

As you're browsing through GospeLink, you may find a passage that you'd like to take with you on your PalmPilot to study at your leisure. You can easily copy that passage to your PalmPilot directly from GospeLink.

TO COPY TEXT TO YOUR PALMPILOT:

1. Select the text you want to copy.

2. Click the text with the right mouse button. A pop-up menu will appear.

3. Click **Copy To . . .** The copy menu will appear.

4. Click **Copy text to PalmPilot.**

A dialog box will appear so you can name the document that will be copied to your PalmPilot.

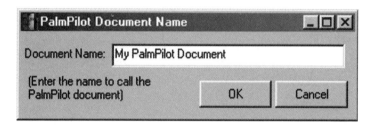

The name you give the document will appear on your PalmPilot, so it should reflect the contents of what is being copied.

GospeLink will then display a standard Windows save dialog box so you can name the file and specify its location. Then you can download the file to your PalmPilot.

TIP: You can copy any text displayed in any of GospeLink's text windows, which means you can copy the scriptures, book passages, or any other text that your PalmPilot will hold. For example, if you've done a search and are showing only search results in the text window, you can copy those results to your PalmPilot to browse at your leisure. If you use the Topic Explorer to display the scripture passages on a certain topic, you can copy that selection of passages to your PalmPilot for your personal study.

SENDING TO PALMPILOT FROM PREPRINT

If you've copied items to PrePrint for printing, you can also send them from PrePrint to your PalmPilot. This is helpful if you have several passages that you'd like to send to PalmPilot, and you'd like to send them all at once.

To copy all the items in the PrePrint list to a document that you can copy to your PalmPilot, click this button on the PrePrint toolbar:

A dialog box will appear, allowing you to name the document.

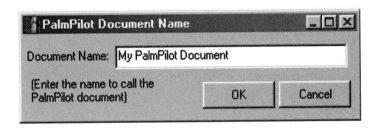

This is the name you will see on your PalmPilot, so the name should reflect the contents of what is being copied.

GospeLink will then display a standard Windows save dialog where you can name the file and specify its location. You can then load the file into your PalmPilot.

SAVING TO PALMPILOT FROM COMPOSER

If you've used Composer to write a talk or lesson, you can save your work to your PalmPilot and use it for reference in church. You can also use Composer as an easy way to copy text from GospeLink to your PalmPilot, whether it is part of a talk or lesson or just for your personal study.

 TO SAVE A FILE FROM COMPOSER TO YOUR PALMPILOT:

1. In Composer, click the **File** menu.
2. Click **Send to PalmPilot.**

A dialog box will appear so you can name the document that will be copied to your PalmPilot.

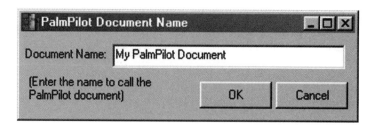

The name you give the document will appear on your PalmPilot, so it should reflect the contents of what is being copied.

GospeLink will then display a standard Windows save dialog box so you can name the file and specify its location. Then you can download the file to your PalmPilot.

TIP: You can use the standard Windows copy commands to copy items from other Windows applications, paste them into Composer, and then save them to your PalmPilot. This feature is extraordinarily powerful. It means you can copy nearly anything to your PalmPilot, including talks and lessons you've written with your regular word processor, pages from the World Wide Web, and many other items.

PART 5: USING THE LDS QUOTATIONS LIBRARY

CHAPTER 33
LDS QUOTATIONS LIBRARY

The LDS Quotations Library lets you quickly find a quotation for a talk, lesson, or other purpose. It includes more than 6,000 quotations, all of which can be viewed by author or topic. It also includes links to several of the tools in GospeLink, including Composer, PrePrint, and various copying options.

QUOTATIONS TOOLBAR

The toolbar for the LDS Quotations Library works like a standard Windows toolbar. To choose a button, simply click it with the mouse. Here are the buttons and what they do:

🏠	Resets the text display to the top of the list and clears all searches.
⇐	Moves the display to the previously found item.
⇒	Moves the display to the next found item.

🖼️	Displays topics in the list.
🗣️	Displays authors in the list.
🖨️	Starts PrePrint in GospeLink.
🖥️	Starts Composer in GospeLink.
📋	Copies text to the Windows Clipboard, Composer, PrePrint, or PalmPilot.
🔍+	Makes the text larger.
🔍-	Makes the text smaller.

QUOTATIONS MENU

The menu for the LDS Quotations Library works like a standard Windows menu and contains many options to help you use the library. To choose a menu item, just click it with your mouse. Here are the menu items and what they do:

 ### FILE

Close	Closes the LDS Quotations Library.

 ### EDIT

Copy	Copies text to the Windows Clipboard, Composer, PrePrint, or PalmPilot.

 ### LISTS

Topics	Displays topics in the list.
Authors	Displays authors in the list.

TOOLS

Composer	Starts Composer in GospeLink.
PrePrint	Starts PrePrint in GospeLink.
Clear Search	Clears the text window of a search.

 HELP

Contents	Displays the LDS Quotations Library Help System.
About	Displays information about the LDS Quotations Library.

SEARCHING QUOTATIONS

To search the LDS Quotations Library, enter the word or phrase you are searching for and click the **Search** button. The text area will then display the first quotation that contains what you are searching for. The found items will be highlighted. You can move from item to item by clicking the **Previous** and **Next** buttons on the toolbar. (These are the arrow buttons pointing left and right.)

If you are searching for a phrase, enclose the phrase in quotation marks.

You can also press the **Enter** key to start your search.

To clear a search, use the **Clear Search** option under the **Tools** menu.

AUTHOR LIST

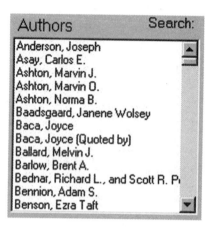

The author list displays all the authors in the Quotations Library in alphabetical order. You can use this list to find quotations by a specific author. Use the scroll bar to scroll through the list. You can also click in the list and then press a letter key to jump to the first author whose last name begins with that letter.

To select an author, click the author's name with the mouse. The selected author will be highlighted, and quotations by that author will appear in the text window.

You can show the author list by:

- Clicking the **Authors** button on the toolbar:

- Choosing the **Authors** option on the **Lists** menu.

TOPIC LIST

The topic list displays all of the topics in the Quotations Library in alphabetical order. This list allows you to find quotations on a specific topic. You can use the scroll bar to scroll through the list. You can also click in the list and then press a letter key to jump to the first topic that begins with that letter. After you choose a topic, the list will expand to show all the authors with a quotation on that topic.

You can show the topics list by:

- Clicking the **Topics** button on the toolbar:

- Choosing the **Topics** option on the **Lists** menu.

 TO SELECT A TOPIC AND AUTHOR:

1. Click the topic you want.
2. Click the author you want.

The selected author will be highlighted, and quotations by that author will appear in the text window.

TEXT WINDOW

The text window is where the quotations actually appear. You can scroll through the quotations and read them, or you can use some of the following tools to help you find a quotation:

Search	Finds words you search for in the LDS Quotations Library. (The search tool is located directly above the text window.)
Author List	Lets you choose an author and see quotations by that author.
Topic List	Lets you choose a topic, then an author.
Browse	Allows you to scroll through the text window and read the quotations.

PRINTING

To print from the LDS Quotations Library, select the text you want to print and then copy it to PrePrint. You can copy many quotations to PrePrint and then print them all at once.

COPYING TEXT

To copy from the LDS Quotations Library, select the text you want to copy and then choose where to copy it. You can copy text to the Windows Clipboard, Composer, PrePrint, or PalmPilot.

You can copy text from the menu, toolbar, or pop-up menu (by clicking the right mouse button).

Part 6: Getting the Most from GospeLink

CHAPTER 34

Writing a Talk

If you need to write a talk, you'll find GospeLink extremely helpful. But first, let's consider what the Lord has to say about speaking: "Seek not to declare my word, but first seek to obtain my word, and then shall your tongue be loosed; then, if you desire, you shall have my Spirit and my word, yea, the power of God unto the convincing of men" (D&C 11:21).

A constant, regular study of the gospel will be invaluable to you as you are called on to speak. As you spend time studying the gospel:

- You will find more things to talk about.
- You will find stories and examples to illustrate your points.
- You will discover new ideas and ways of thinking about things.
- Most important, studying the gospel will help bring the companionship of the Spirit so you can speak "unto the convincing of men."

Can you use GospeLink to help you obtain the Lord's word? Yes, in many ways. GospeLink is a tool you can use both in your study of the gospel and in specific tasks, such as preparing a talk.

For ideas about how to use GospeLink to study the gospel, see pages 221–48.

A Simple Outline

Let's suppose you've been assigned to give a talk on the subject of faith. How can you use GospeLink to help you prepare?

One way to prepare a talk is to use a simple outline. You use an outline to organize your talk just as you use the format of a sonnet to write a sonnet, or the format of a symphony to compose a symphony. Using an outline can actually improve a talk by giving it a structure that make sense and flows naturally from beginning to end. One such outline is this:

1. Opening remarks
2. Story
3. Quotation or scripture
4. Poem
5. Closing testimony

It's up to you to decide what you want to say in your talk. But using an outline makes structuring your remarks and tying them together easy. For your opening remarks, your remarks about the story and the quotation, and your closing testimony, you'll have to rely on yourself and the Lord (with the help of all that gospel study you've been doing). But for the story, quotation or scripture, and poem, GospeLink can help you a lot.

STORY

Since your talk will be on faith, you can start by using GospeLink to find a story about faith. There are various ways to do this. A good way is to open GospeLink Explorer and click on the **Stories/Poems** tab. In the window on the left are dozens of topics. Click on the **Faith** folder, then on the **Stories** folder, and you will see a list of twenty-six stories about faith. You can click on a story to preview it in the window on the right. After looking at a few stories, you will probably find one you think is just right, for example, "Faith of a Child," by Heber C. Kimball. Click the **Go To** button to open the story in the Books window. Then select the story and copy it to Composer. (See Stories/Poems Explorer on pages 155–58.)

QUOTATION OR SCRIPTURE

Now you need a quotation about faith. The easiest way to find one is to start the LDS Quotations Library. Click on the topic of faith and browse through the quotations until you find one you like. Copy the quotation to Composer (see pages 168–74).

You can also use GospeLink to find scriptures on your topic. To do so, use the Topics tab in GospeLink Explorer. (See Topic Explorer on pages 115–17 and Scriptures window on pages 53–60.)

POEM

Finally, you need a poem. Again open GospeLink Explorer and click on the **Stories/Poems** tab. Again click on the **Faith** folder, but this time click on **Poems.** Sixteen poems are listed in this category. Look through the poems to find one you want. For example, you could use "Ballad of the Tempest," by James Thomas Fields, which ties in nicely with the story you selected earlier. Again, copy it to Composer.

USING COMPOSER

Now go into Composer, where you will see, in order, the story, quotation, and poem you selected. Tie together the elements of your talk by doing the following:

*   In front of the story, make a brief note about what you want to say in your opening remarks.
*   After the story, type in your remarks about the story.
*   After the quotation, type in your remarks about it.
*   And finally, after the poem, sketch out what you want to say in your closing testimony.

    That's it! You've got a good talk that teaches something about faith, using material that most people should find quite interesting.

A LONGER TALK

You can use the same techniques to write a longer talk, too. If your talk is going to be about several different subjects, you might try an outline like this:

1. Opening remarks
2. Story on topic 1
3. Quotation on topic 1
4. Story on topic 2
5. Scripture on topic 2
6. Poem
7. Closing testimony

If your talk has to be longer but all on one subject, you might try an outline like this:

1. Opening remarks
2. Story
3. Quotation
4. Story
5. Scripture
6. Poem

7. Closing testimony

You can rearrange things in the way that seems best, using GospeLink to help you find the material you need. Above all, think things through, pray about what you're doing, and rely on the Spirit of the Lord. Then you'll give your talk as the Lord wants you to.

For more information about how to write and give a talk, see *You Can Learn to Speak,* by Royal Garff, which is included in GospeLink.

LEARNING MORE ABOUT GIVING A TALK

For more information about giving a talk, you can use GospeLink to study the scriptures that have to do with speaking. You can also use the Comprehensive Index in GospeLink to learn more about speaking.

 TO STUDY THE SCRIPTURES ABOUT SPEAKING:

1. Start GospeLink Explorer by clicking the **Explorer** button on the main toolbar.

2. Click the **Topics** tab.

3. Click the **S** alphabet button.

4. Click one of the topics under **Speaking,** such as "Holy Ghost, Mission of."

5. Study the scriptures displayed in the window on the right, taking notes about how you might apply what they have to say.

 TO USE THE COMPREHENSIVE INDEX TO LEARN MORE ABOUT SPEAKING:

1. Start GospeLink Explorer by clicking the **Explorer** button on the main toolbar.

2. Click the **Index** tab.

3. Type the word *speaking* in the search box at the bottom of the screen.

4. Click the **Search** button.

5. Click the **S** alphabet button.

6. Click the right mouse button in the Comprehensive Index window on the left.

7. Click **Next Match.**

8. Repeat steps 6 and 7 until you see the long list of topics that begins with the word *Speaking.*

9. Browse through the topics until you see one that looks interesting.

10. Click one of the book titles under the topic.

You can preview the book passage on that topic in the right window, or you can click the **Go To** button to go to the passage in the book.

CHAPTER 35
PREPARING A LESSON

Preparing a lesson is a lot like writing a talk. Again, the most important thing is to be *personally* prepared and to rely on the Lord. After that, GospeLink can help you in a variety of ways.

As with writing a talk, it's often a good idea to use a general outline to help you prepare your lesson. Here's what such an outline might look like:

1. Attention-getter
2. Scripture reading and discussion
3. Stories and discussion
4. Quotation or poem
5. Closing testimony

Different lessons will rely more heavily on different parts of the outline. For example, in a Gospel Doctrine lesson a large part of your time will probably be spent in reading and discussing the scriptures, whereas in a Primary lesson you will probably spend more time on stories and discussion as well as other activities. Use and adapt the information in this section in the way that will best apply to you and the lesson you are preparing.

The Church's lesson manuals are excellent tools and should be used as the basis for your Church lessons. Still, *how* you do that is a matter of individual inspiration, and we hope you'll find GospeLink useful as you fit each lesson to the needs of your particular class.

ATTENTION-GETTER

It's almost always a good idea to begin your lesson with something that gets the class's attention and prepares them for what the lesson will be about. You can use all kinds of different things as attention-getters:

- Physical objects
- Musical selections
- Pictures
- Puzzles
- Intriguing questions
- Short selections from a videotape
- Short selections from an audiotape
- Stories

- Poems
- Quotations

and many more. You can use almost anything as long as it's appropriate, intriguing, and pertinent to the lesson. Your lesson manual probably includes some ideas about attention-getters for the particular lesson you're teaching.

GospeLink is especially helpful for finding stories, quotations, scriptures, poems, and so on, as explained in the section on writing a talk. It can also help you with specific ideas and suggestions about teaching in such books as *Teach Ye Diligently,* by Boyd K. Packer, and *Raising Up a Family to the Lord,* by Gene R. Cook.

SCRIPTURE READING AND DISCUSSION

Scripture reading is important in teaching a lesson because the curriculum of the Church is based on the scriptures. Some teachers are afraid to read from the scriptures in class. Don't be! The scriptures are the word of the Lord, and if you read them with understanding, and with discussion from class members, they can be powerful tools in teaching the principles of the gospel.

GospeLink is unsurpassed in helping you understand the scriptures. For starters, you can use the Cross-References tab in the References window to see all of the book passages that comment on a verse you've selected in the Scriptures window (see page 69). You can also read the numerous scripture commentaries included with GospeLink. To find them:

1. Start GospeLink Explorer.
2. Click the **Subjects** tab.
3. Click the **S** alphabet button.
4. Click **Scripture Commentary.**

You'll see dozens of books that comment on the scriptures, which you can use to understand the scripture passages for your current lesson.

GospeLink is a great tool for scripture study for many other reasons, including quick cross-references to other scriptures, side-by-side comparisons, parallel passages, Strong's Greek and Hebrew dictionaries, and Topic Explorer. To learn the many ways you can use GospeLink to study your scriptures, see the Scriptures window section on pages 53–60, the References window section on pages 65–74, the Scripture Explorer section on pages 108–14, and the Topic Explorer section on pages 115–17.

Once you understand the scriptures for your lesson, you'll feel much more comfortable discussing them. As you read them in class, don't be afraid to stop in the middle of a verse and comment on it, or better yet, ask an open-ended question about it so that class members can comment. For example, you might ask, "What does that phrase mean to you?" or "What do you think Paul is trying to teach us in this verse?" Notice that these questions have no "right" or "wrong" answer. They are simply a way to get class members to look into their minds and hearts and to share their ideas.

The Holy Ghost is our true teacher, and through his inspiration we actually teach each other during the class. The Lord explained it this way: "Appoint among yourselves a teacher, and let not all be spokesmen at once; but let one speak at a time and let all listen unto his sayings, that when all have spoken that all may be edified of all, and that every man may have an equal privilege" (D&C 88:122). That takes a lot of pressure off you as the teacher. It means you don't have to know everything and don't have to explain everything, and it means the Lord is in charge of the class, which is as it should be.

STORIES AND DISCUSSION

As you saw in the chapter on preparing a talk, GospeLink can help you find a wide variety of stories and examples to use in your lesson. In writing a talk, you used the Stories/Poems tab in GospeLink Explorer to do this. In preparing a lesson, you may want to use Scripture Sets. Scripture Sets are collections of stories, miracles, and parables from the scriptures themselves. To use them:

1. Start GospeLink Explorer.

2. Click the **Scriptures** tab.

3. Select a Scripture Set from the list of Scripture Sets, such as **New Testament: Stories.**

4. Click on a story you think might be interesting, such as "Feeding the Five Thousand."

The story will be displayed in the window on the right, and you can go to it in the scriptures by clicking the **Go To** button. (To learn more about using Scripture Sets, see the section about them on pages 112–13.)

You can use this story and others in teaching the lesson. In addition, however, try using the story as a springboard to get class members to relate examples from their own lives. You can do this by reading the story and then asking an open-ended question like this:

"Have any of you had an experience something like this?" or "Have any of you had an experience where your prayers were answered in an unusual way?"

Then be quiet and wait. Don't be too quick to jump in with your own answer. After a few moments, a class member will probably respond with a story you could never have anticipated. This is the kind of thing that really brings the gospel to life—and your lesson as well. Not only that, but what the class member is really doing is bearing testimony, whether anyone realizes it or not. When people bear testimony, the Holy Ghost bears witness of that testimony. And when the Holy Ghost bears witness, that's when learning really occurs—which is what teaching the gospel is all about.

Another wonderful thing about using stories, either from the scriptures or from the class members themselves, is that you can use them to help class members learn specific principles of the gospel. For example, you might say, "What principles can we learn about prayer from the story of the loaves and fishes?" or "What things did Sister Hernandez do to increase her faith?" Notice, again, that these questions are open-ended and that they ask for multiple responses: "What principles?" "What things?" Such questions encourage responses from class members because they have no "wrong" answers. Any sincere answer is acceptable. Any sincere answer is also valuable, because it offers an insight into the gospel that the class may not have had before. Notice how different this is from seeing the teacher as the dispenser of knowledge. Instead, the teacher is simply a facilitator, someone who guides and encourages the discussion.

When class members start giving their answers to such questions, write their answers in summary form on the chalkboard so they can see them as well as hear them, which will help them retain the information. This is another way of demonstrating to the class that what they have to say is important, and it encourages additional discussion. Finally, at the end of your lesson, you'll have a wonderful list of gospel principles that class members can use in their lives and that you can use to summarize the discussion.

QUOTATION OR POEM

Using a quotation or poem is a good way to end your lesson. It's a way of restating what the lesson was about, and it often helps people *feel* as well as understand the importance of the principle that was taught. It's also a natural way to lead into your closing testimony. You can use

GospeLink to find all kinds of useful quotations and inspiring poems that will greatly add to your lesson. (See Stories/Poems Explorer on pages 155–58.)

LEARNING MORE ABOUT TEACHING A LESSON

For more information on preparing and teaching a lesson, you can use GospeLink to study scriptures and read books that have to do with teaching. You can also use GospeLink's Comprehensive Index to learn more about teaching.

 TO STUDY THE SCRIPTURES ABOUT TEACHING:

1. Start GospeLink Explorer by clicking the **Explorer** button on the main toolbar.
2. Click the **Topics** tab.
3. Click the **T** alphabet button.
4. Click one of the topics under **Teaching** or **Teaching with the Spirit**.
5. Study the scriptures displayed in the window on the right, taking notes about how you might apply what they have to say.

 TO READ A BOOK ABOUT TEACHING:

1. Start GospeLink Explorer by clicking the **Explorer** button on the main toolbar.
2. Click the **Subjects** tab.
3. Click the **T** alphabet button.
4. Click **Teaching**.
5. Click the title of a book that looks interesting.
6. Click the **Go To** button.

You can read the book, highlight meaningful passages, and figure out ways to incorporate its ideas into your own teaching style.

 TO USE THE COMPREHENSIVE INDEX TO LEARN MORE ABOUT TEACHING:

1. Start GospeLink Explorer by clicking the **Explorer** button on the main toolbar.
2. Click the **Index** tab.
3. Type the word *teaching* in the search box at the bottom of the screen.
4. Click the **Search** button.

5. Click the **T** alphabet button.

6. Click the right mouse button in the Comprehensive Index window on the left.

7. Click **Next Match.**

8. Repeat steps 6 and 7 until you see the long list of topics that begins with the word *Teaching.*

9. Browse through the topics until you see one that looks interesting.

10. Click one of the book titles under the topic.

You can preview the book passage on that topic in the right window, or you can go to the passage in the book by clicking the **Go To** button. As you go through several of these passages, you'll find a wealth of information to help you.

CHAPTER 36
PREPARING A FAMILY HOME EVENING

Preparing a lesson for family home evening is not much different from preparing any other lesson (see pages 210–15). However, GospeLink includes some features you may find particularly useful in teaching your family:

• Scripture Sets.

Use scripture sets to find dozens of stories from the scriptures that you can read and discuss together. This works well with children of all ages, because you can gear your discussion questions to the age of your children. If you have small children, for example, you can ask simple, factual questions, such as "What did Jesus do for his friend Lazarus?" or "What did the disciples catch in their nets?" Older children can answer more complex questions: "How did Jesus feel about Lazarus's death? How do you know? Why do you think he felt that way?" or "Why do you think the disciples were willing to try catching fish again when they hadn't caught anything all night?" If you have children of various ages, you can direct different questions to different children. As in teaching lessons in Church, be open to various answers, not just the one you have in mind. Those unexpected answers may be the key to learning what the Lord wants you to learn in your home.

• The Stories/Poems tab in GospeLink Explorer.

Use the Stories/Poems tab in GospeLink Explorer to find all kinds of stories by subject. If you're teaching a lesson on prayer, for example, you'll find several stories from Church history on prayer that you can read and discuss together. One particularly effective way to use stories—including stories from the scriptures—is to give your family something to think about before you read, so they can be looking for it while you read the story. For example, you might say, "As we read this story, see if you can tell how Jesus felt about his friend Lazarus." After reading, you'll find that your discussion of the story is much richer than it would have been, and your family will have been more involved during the reading of the story. (You can also use this technique in lessons at Church.)

• Books with stories that are especially useful for families.

GospeLink includes many books with stories that are great for families. Some of these include *Missionary Stories, We'll Bring the World His Truth, A String of Pearls, Early Scenes in Church History, Gems for the Young Folks,* and *Leaves from My Journal.*

• Books that explain how to hold family home evenings.

GospeLink includes several books that offer all kinds of suggestions on how to hold and improve family home evenings. In particular, you may want to look at *Raising Up a Family to the Lord,* by Gene R. Cook, and *You, Your Family, and the Scriptures,* by Ed J. Pinegar.

 TO LEARN MORE ABOUT PREPARING AND GIVING FAMILY HOME EVENING LESSONS:

Use GospeLink to find more information on preparing and giving lessons for family home evening. One way to do this is by looking up information in the Comprehensive Index.

1. Start GospeLink Explorer by clicking the **Explorer** button on the main toolbar.

2. Click the **Index** tab.

3. Type *family home evening* in the search box at the bottom of the screen.

4. Click the **Search** button.

5. Click the **F** alphabet button.

6. Click the right mouse button in the Comprehensive Index window on the left.

7. Click **Next Match.**

8. Repeat steps 6 and 7 until you see the list of topics that begins with the words *family home evening.*

9. Browse through the topics until you see one that looks interesting.

10. Click one of the book titles under the topic.

Now you can preview the book passage on that topic in the right window or click the **Go To** button to go to the passage in the Books window. As you go through several of these passages, you'll find a wealth of information to make your family home evenings fun and effective.

TIP: For older children, you may want to take one or more family home evening lessons to teach them how to use GospeLink. You can set up each child as a GospeLink user and show them how some of GospeLink's features work. As you teach your children how to use GospeLink, you will see how it can become an important tool in helping your family learn the gospel.

CHAPTER 37
PERSONALIZING THE LIBRARY

You probably enjoy marking and making notes in the printed books on your bookshelf. It can help you learn and retain the information you read. With GospeLink you can highlight and make notes in the same way, only better, by using bookmarks, highlighting, and personal text notes. These can be unique for each GospeLink user on your computer. (See the Highlight section on pages 175–76, the Bookmarks section on pages 177–78, and the Personal Text Notes section on pages 38–39.) These personalizations will be preserved if you save your work before you exit GospeLink. (For more information see the Save section on page 193.)

BOOKMARKS

You can use bookmarks to mark your place in GospeLink as you read or as you find passages you want to come back to. There are several nice things about doing this in GospeLink:

- Your bookmarks won't fall out on the floor, as they can with a printed book.
- You can have as many different bookmarks as you want, and they'll never be in your way.
- You can find, move, rename, or delete bookmarks.

Don't be afraid to use bookmarks freely. You'll find them very helpful.

TIP: While preparing a lesson, have you ever run across a great quotation that you can't use now but would be perfect for your lesson in several weeks? Use a bookmark to mark that quotation. You can even name the bookmark with the date when you'll use it, for example, "April 6, 1999," or with a name like "Quotation for lesson on Matthew 24." Then, when it's time for your lesson, look back through your bookmarks to find the passage you've previously marked.

For instructions on how to use bookmarks, see pages 177–78.

HIGHLIGHTING

You can also use highlighting to mark passages you want to find again. However, you can use highlighting for other purposes as well, such as:

- Marking passages on certain topics, using a different color for each topic.
- Marking passages that are particularly important to you.
- Marking passages that you want to search all at one time.

For instructions on how to highlight, see the Highlight section on pages 175–76.

For instructions on how to search highlighting, see pages 78–79.

TIP: If you don't include words to search for, you can find *all* of your highlighted text at once.

For more information about how to use highlighting, see *Marking the Scriptures,* by Daniel H. Ludlow, which is included in GospeLink.

PERSONAL TEXT NOTES

Making personal text notes is like making notes in the margins of a book. It lets you add your own thoughts and commentary to what you are reading. The notes are attached to the library text where you make them; the next time you read that text, you can see what you had to say the last time you read it, and you can also edit or add to your previous notes. You may want to type in the current date with each note so you can see how your insights have grown over time. In fact, you can use personal text notes as a sort of study journal as you study the scriptures and other materials. Later, you can search the library for text you've entered in the notes.

For instructions on how to use personal text notes, see pages 38–39.

For instructions on how to search personal text notes, see pages 78–79.

TIP: If you don't include words to search for, you can find *all* of your personal text notes. You'll need to close each note after you're finished reading it; then click the **Next** button to open the next note that was found.

CHAPTER 38
RESEARCHING THE LIBRARY

Although you may use GospeLink simply for reading, much of the time you'll probably use it to find specific information for a talk, a lesson, a writing project—in short, for research. Maybe you're looking for the answer to a particular gospel question, or maybe you're looking for a quotation that you need but can only vaguely remember. In either case, GospeLink can help.

RESEARCHING A QUOTATION

If you're using GospeLink for research, you may want to vary your approach depending on what you're looking for. For example, let's say you're looking for a quotation. Maybe you can't remember exactly what was said, but you do remember that the speaker was a member of a handcart company and that he said something about coming to know God in his "extremities"—and that's the one specific word you remember. In a case like that, you might want to try searching the entire library for that word. (For information on searching, see pages 77–86.)

If you search the entire library for the word *extremities* with Disk A of GospeLink, you'll get thirty-two matches in books by General Authorities. Then, if you look at the first match, you'll see this quotation: "Francis Webster, a member of the Martin Handcart Company, stated, 'Every one of us came through with the absolute knowledge that God lives for we became acquainted with him in our extremities.'"

And that's the very quotation you needed! So if you're looking for something very specific, down to a word or phrase, a search may be the most effective research tool you can use.

There is one caution with this approach, however: When doing a search, try to use words or phrases that are unique or at least unusual. For example, *extremities* is not a word that is commonly used, which made finding the quotation quite easy. But if you had searched for the word *pioneers,* you would have found 705 matches in books by General Authorities and 1,239 matches in books by other LDS authors. Looking through all of those matches for the quotation would have been next to impossible. The goal is to search for a word or phrase that will lead you to what you're looking for with as few "hits," or matches, as possible. For example, the phrase *in our extremities* would have been even better than just the word *extremities* because that word combination is less likely to be found than the word *extremities* alone.

Remember that there are many ways to narrow your search with the various options in the Search window (see pages 78–80), with Folio advanced searching (see pages 44–48), and with the different ways of searching on the tabs in GospeLink Explorer.

RESEARCHING FOR A TALK OR LESSON

Now let's say you need to do a different kind of research—you're looking for information for a talk or lesson on a specific topic, such as charity. In that case, a search would be one of the worst ways to find information. That is because if you did a search for the word *charity*, you'd get 1,073 matches in books by General Authorities alone, with 3,130 matches in books by other LDS authors. It would be almost impossible to ever look through all of those books; such an approach would not necessarily give you the most useful information first, either.

A better approach to finding information by topic would be using GospeLink Explorer. Here are some ways you might do that:

- Look through the Scripture Sets on the Scriptures tab for scriptural stories that have to do with charity. For example, if you looked through the New Testament: Parables set, you'd see such stories as the Good Samaritan, the Prodigal Son, the Mote and Beam, and the Unmerciful Servant, any of which could be used in a talk on charity. (For more information on Scripture Sets, see pages 112–13.)
- Use the Topics tab to see scriptures about charity (see pages 115–17). Here you'll find some excellent scripture passages you could use as a starting point for a talk or in the body of your talk. Also, by thinking about some of these scriptures, you may find yourself coming up with a new viewpoint about charity that would make your talk especially interesting and helpful to people.
- Use the Subjects tab to find books on your subject (see pages 133–36). Looking through those books will help you find all kinds of ideas, quotations, and stories you could use in a lesson or a talk.
- Use the Stories/Poems tab to find stories and poems that have to do with charity (see pages 155–58). Using a story or poem is an

excellent way to start or end a talk, and a story or poem may also give you ideas about the points you want to make in your talk.

- Use the Type of Talk list on the Talks tab to display a list of talks that have to do with charity (see page 145). By reading through some of these talks, you'll see the approach various General Authorities have taken in talking about charity, and you'll also see all of the stories, examples, poems, and scriptures they used to illustrate their points. This is a wealth of information for anyone giving a talk or lesson.
- Use the Ensign Index tab to list *Ensign* articles on the subject of charity (see pages 162–67). Then you can read those articles in the *Ensign* itself, either your own or those in your ward library.
- Use the Index tab to pinpoint specific information about charity in the LDS books in GospeLink (see pages 137–41). The Index tab makes it possible to get a broad overview of information about a topic and then go to specific book passages that discuss that topic.

Here's a summary of kinds of information you may want to find and some of the best ways to find that information in GospeLink:

Specific words or phrases	Search
Specific information in books	Index tab in GospeLink Explorer
Books by a specific title	Books tab in GospeLink Explorer
Books by a specific author	Author tab in GospeLink Explorer
Books by a type of author	Type of Author list on the Author tab in GospeLink Explorer
Books on a specific subject	Subject tab in GospeLink Explorer
Scriptures on a specific topic	Topics tab in GospeLink Explorer

Scripture stories	Scripture Sets on the Scriptures tab in GospeLink Explorer
Stories or poems on a specific subject	Stories/Poems tab in GospeLink Explorer
Talks on a specific subject	Type of Talk list on the Talks tab in GospeLink Explorer
Talks by a specific speaker	Speaker tab in GospeLink Explorer
Talks by a type of speaker	Type of Speaker list on the Speaker tab in GospeLink Explorer

RESEARCHING SOURCES

If you're a writer or editor, you may want to use GospeLink to find specific page numbers and publication information. GospeLink can help you to some extent in this way. You can identify author and title in the reference area of a text window (see pages 37–38). Page numbers are usually shown in the display label above a text window. Also, when you copy text to Composer, the title and page number will be displayed above the text in Composer.

TIP: If you need more publication information about a specific book, you might want to try finding it through Brigham Young University's online card catalog. To use the catalog, point your Internet browser to www.lib.byu.edu and click on "BYU Library."

GETTING ANSWERS

At times you may look to GospeLink as a possible place to find answers to questions or problems you are having in your life. If you want to use GospeLink in this way, there are some places you should definitely look.

The first place is the Topics tab in GospeLink Explorer (see pages 115–17), which will guide you to scriptures on various topics, such as money management or parenting or repentance.

If you have questions about specific scripture passages, you can use the References window to see commentary that various Church leaders and writers have provided about that passage (see pages 69–70).

Another place you might look is the Index tab in GospeLink Explorer (see pages 137–41), where you'll find index entries for literally thousands of gospel topics. You can browse through these topics and go to the passages that discuss a topic of your choice.

GospeLink includes a wide variety of books on gospel living, family life, self-help, and so on, as well as books on Church doctrine and history and even books that offer answers to gospel questions, such as *Answers to Gospel Questions,* by Joseph Fielding Smith; *Evidences and Reconciliations,* by John A. Widtsoe; and *The Doctrine and Covenants: A Book of Answers.* You might also try finding answers to difficult questions and problems by looking on the Subjects tab of GospeLink Explorer for books on the subject of apologetics (books that defend the Church), doctrine, family and parenthood, gospel living, self-help, and many others.

If any of these tools help you find answers or help with a troublesome problem or question, all of the work that went into GospeLink will have been worthwhile. We hope you will find GospeLink useful in this way.

GospeLink is one avenue of finding answers, but as with other important or difficult questions or problems, it may help to talk with your family, friends, Church leaders, or professional counselors. In addition, remember that there are gospel questions for which answers have not yet been made known: "We believe that [God] will yet reveal many great and important things pertaining to the Kingdom of God" (Article of Faith 9; see also D&C 101:32–34).

LEARNING MORE ABOUT FINDING ANSWERS TO QUESTIONS AND SOLVING PROBLEMS

Use GospeLink to find more information on getting answers to questions and problems. There are several ways to do this:

 TO STUDY THE SCRIPTURES ON VARIOUS TOPICS:

1. Start GospeLink Explorer by clicking the **Explorer** button on the main toolbar.

2. Click the **Topics** tab.

3. Click the **P** alphabet button.

4. Click one of the topics under "Problem-Solving."

5. Study the scriptures in the window on the right, taking notes about how you might apply what they have to say.

You might also want to try the same procedure for the topic of prayer or for a specific topic you have questions about.

 TO READ A BOOK ABOUT HOW TO SOLVE PROBLEMS OR FIND ANSWERS:

1. Start GospeLink Explorer by clicking the **Explorer** button on the main toolbar.

2. Click the **Subjects** tab.

3. Using the alphabet tabs, look through books on such subjects as self-help, prayer, counseling, and so on.

You can read a book, highlight meaningful passages, and make notes about how to apply what you learn.

 TO USE THE COMPREHENSIVE INDEX TO LEARN MORE ABOUT HOW TO SOLVE PROBLEMS OR FIND ANSWERS:

1. Start GospeLink Explorer by clicking the **Explorer** button on the main toolbar.

2. Click the **Index** tab.

3. Use the search box, alphabet buttons, and right mouse button to find such topics as problem-solving, prayer, questions, counseling, and so on. You might also try looking for information on a specific question or problem.

4. Browse through the topics until you see one that looks interesting.

5. Click one of the book titles under the topic.

Now you can preview the book passage on that topic in the right window or click the Go To button to go to the passage in the Books window. As you go through several of these passages, you may find information to help you with your questions or problems.

CHAPTER 39
READING THE LIBRARY

READING FROM START TO FINISH

Hugh Nibley, the eminent LDS scholar, claims to have obtained his doctorate at Berkeley by reading his way through the university library. He writes, "I [started] in the stacks beginning at the southwest corner of the ninth level and working down to the northeast corner of the first level, book by book, stopping whenever something significant caught my eye" (*Nibley on the Timely and the Timeless* [Provo: BYU Religious Studies Center, 1978], xxii). You can read the GospeLink library in the same way; just start with the first book and read whatever looks interesting until you get to the end. This will keep you busy for a long time, and when you're finished, you'll have quite an education.

If you're interested in using this approach, you'll probably want to do the following:
- Set the Books window to full screen (see pages 28–30).
- Use the table of contents to browse through books and read them (see pages 40–42).
- Use a bookmark to mark your place (see pages 177–78).
- Use personal text notes to keep track of your thoughts about what you're reading (see pages 38–39).
- Use the Personal Notes view in the References window to keep track of what you've read (see pages 70–71).

READING AT RANDOM

Another way to approach an electronic reference library is to browse through it at random, find a book that looks interesting, start reading, and see where it will lead you. Over time, you can learn a great deal in this way. This approach is illustrated in the story of an obscure woman who insisted that she "never had a chance." One night she muttered these words to Dr. Louis Agassiz, the distinguished naturalist, after one of his lectures in London. He replied, "You say, madam, you never had a chance? What do you do?"

"I am single and help my sister run a boarding house."

"What do you do?" he asked again.

"I skin potatoes and chop onions."

He said, "Where do you sit during these interesting but homely duties?"

"On the bottom steps of the kitchen stairs."

"Where do your feet rest?"

"On the glazed bricks."

"What is a glazed brick?"

"I don't know, sir."

He said, "How long have you been sitting there?"

"Fifteen years."

"Madam, here is my personal card. Would you kindly write me concerning the nature of a glazed brick."

She went home and explored the dictionary to discover that a brick was a piece of baked clay. That definition seemed too simple to send to Dr. Agassiz, so after the dishes were washed, she went to the library and read that a glazed brick is vitrified kaolin and hydrous-aluminum silicate. She didn't know what that meant, but she was curious and found out. Later, she went to a brickyard, where one of the workers told her the history of more than 120 kinds of bricks and tiles and why there have to be so many. Then she sat down and wrote thirty-six pages on the subject of glazed bricks and tiles. Back came a letter from Louis Agassiz: "Dear Madam: This is the best article I have ever seen on the subject. If you will kindly change the three words marked with an asterisk, I will have it published and pay you for it."

A short time later there came a letter that brought $250, and on the bottom of this letter was penciled this query: "What was under those bricks?" She answered with a single word, "Ants." He wrote back and said, "Tell me about the ants." And away she went. She had learned how to learn.

If you'd like to use a similar system, you may want to try the following:

- Use the Subjects tab in GospeLink Explorer to find books on a particular topic (see pages 133–36).
- Use the Index tab in GospeLink Explorer to find passages on a particular topic (see pages 137–41).
- Use the "Book and Chapter Title" Search Set to find books and chapters on a particular topic (see page 80).

READING FROM A SUGGESTED LIST

You can learn a lot by reading at random, but you may be interested in a more structured approach. If so, you can follow one of the suggested reading lists in appendix 1 of this book. These lists don't include everything in GospeLink—far from it. But they do include some of the books we have found especially useful and informative, organized by subject to provide some guidance in how to approach this massive collection.

GOSPEL READING GUIDE

The gospel reading guide in appendix 1 contains several plans for studying the gospel, including:

- *Doctrines of the Gospel.* Includes important doctrinal works from the beginning of the Church to the present.
- *Gospel Living.* Lists books that give practical advice on how to better live the gospel from day to day.
- *History of the Church.* Includes important works about Church history.
- *Lives of the Prophets.* Includes biographies and essays on presidents of the Church.
- *Self-Help and Inspiration.* Lists books that will help you grow emotionally and spiritually, arranged by topic.
- *Studying the Scriptures.* Includes commentaries on the scriptures, both ancient and modern.
- *Women's Interests.* Lists books of special interest to women.
- *Words of the Prophets.* Includes books by presidents of the Church, from Joseph Smith to our current president.

WORLD CLASSICS READING GUIDE

The World Classics Library on GospeLink is a collection of books that many have recognized as enduring works of literature, philosophy, religion, history, and so on, from ancient times to modern. If you're interested in a guide to reading the World Classics Library, you'll find a list in appendix 2 with the works arranged by subject, such as religion, philosophy, inspiration, biography, and so on.

READING WITH PURPOSE

You can also use GospeLink as you would a physical library that has bound books on the shelf and a card catalog listing books by subject, title, and author. Let's say you're interested in learning more about sanctification. Click the Explorer button, then the Subject tab. You'll see a list of subjects, just as you would in the card catalog of a real library. If you click *Sanctification,* you'll see, in alphabetical order, the books in GospeLink that are primarily about that topic. As you click on the books in the list, in the right window you'll see a summary or description of the book. As you browse through the information about the various books, you'll probably see a book that catches your interest—one you'd like to read.

SURVEYING A BOOK

Once you've selected a book you'd like to read, take time to get an overview of the book. You might want to start with the title page, which most people just skip over.

 ### TITLE PAGE

Often the title page reveals important information about the scope and subject of the book. For example, let's consider the title page of a book popularly known as *The Articles of Faith*, by James E. Talmage. The title page says:

A Study of the

Articles of Faith

Being a Consideration of the Principal Doctrines of The Church of Jesus Christ of Latter-day Saints

Now you know that the book is much more than just a discussion about the Articles of Faith. It is a *study* of the Articles of Faith, and its focus is on the *principal doctrines* of the Church. Thus, it would make an excellent book for someone investigating the Church, a new member, or someone who simply wanted to review the basic doctrines of the gospel. But you might not have known that so readily if you hadn't looked at the title page.

 ### AUTHORS

Similarly, as you look at a book you're interested in reading, you should consider the authors. Who are they? What credentials do they have? Let's consider another gospel classic, *Jesus the Christ*. The title page informs us that the author is (again) James E. Talmage, "One of the Twelve Apostles of the Church of Jesus Christ of Latter-day Saints." This alone tells us that the book is worth our time. If we read the first page of the preface, we will also see that Elder Talmage wrote the book "under request and appointment from the presiding authorities of the Church; and the completed work has been read to and is approved by the First Presidency and the Council of the Twelve." Not only that, but the title page informs us that the book was "published by the Church." Taken together, these facts indicate that *Jesus the Christ* is no ordinary book, and that it definitely merits our attention as an important book for gospel study.

Studying the words of the prophets, particularly our current leaders, is important and should be a priority. As President Wilford Woodruff once said, "I will refer to a certain meeting I attended in the town of Kirtland in my early days. At that meeting some remarks were made that have been made here today, with regard to the living oracles and with regard to the written word of God. The same principle was presented, although not as extensively as it has been here, when a leading man in the Church got up and talked upon the subject, and said: 'You have got the word of God before you here in the Bible, Book of Mormon, and Doctrine and Covenants; you have the written word of God, and you who give revelations should give revelations according to those books, as what is written in those books is the word of God. We should confine ourselves to them.' When he concluded, Brother Joseph turned to Brother Brigham Young and said, 'Brother Brigham I want you to take the stand and tell us your views with regard to the written oracles and the written word of God.' Brother Brigham took the stand, and he took the Bible, and laid it down; he took the Book of Mormon, and laid it down; and he took the Book of Doctrine and Covenants, and laid it down before him, and he said: 'There is the written word of God to us, concerning the work of God from the beginning of the world, almost, to our day.' 'And now,' said he, 'when compared with the living oracles those books are nothing to me; those books do not convey the word of God direct to us now, as do the words of a Prophet or a man bearing the Holy Priesthood in our day and generation. I would rather have the living oracles than all the writing in the books.' That was the course he pursued. When he was through, Brother Joseph said to the congregation: 'Brother Brigham has told you the word of the Lord, and he has told you the truth'" (Conference Reports, Oct. 1897, pp. 18–19).

Studying the words of the prophets is vital, but others, too, have important things to say. As President Woodruff also noted, "Whenever the Lord requires any Prophet, Seer, Revelator, Apostle or leading man of the Church to speak, the Spirit of the Lord is with him to give counsel to the people from time to time as he is moved upon, and such as the people ought to hear. But I want you to understand this one thing: the Holy Priesthood and power of God do not stop there; it does not stop with the Presidency, it does not stop with the Twelve Apostles, it does not stop with our leading men of Israel; there is not a man on God's footstool that is sent forth into the world to preach the Gospel but ought to have the Spirit of the Lord upon him and the revelation of God to him" (Conference Reports, Oct. 1897, p. 19).

Others, too, may speak or write by the power of inspiration. When the Angel Moroni visited Joseph Smith, he quoted Joel 2:28–32. The passage begins, "I will pour out my spirit upon all flesh; and your sons and your daughters shall prophesy, your old men shall dream dreams, your young men shall see visions: and also upon the servants and upon the handmaids in those days will I pour out my spirit." Similarly Alma taught, "[God] imparteth his word by angels unto men, yea, not only men but women also. Now this is not all; little children do have words given unto them many times, which confound the wise and the learned" (Alma 32:23).

We may find truth in many places. But on the other hand, just because someone says or writes something doesn't mean it is true. Latter-day Saints who find some intriguing and unusual doctrine in the *Journal of Discourses,* for example, shouldn't just automatically accept it as gospel truth without first seeing how it fits with stated Church doctrine and the teachings of the living prophet. In August 1913, the First Presidency sent out a letter to members of the Church, warning, "Anything at discord with that which comes from God through the [current] head of the Church is not to be received as authoritative or reliable. In secular as well as spiritual affairs, Saints may receive Divine guidance and revelation affecting themselves, but this does not convey authority to direct others, and is not to be accepted when contrary to Church covenants, doctrine or discipline, or to known facts, demonstrated truths, or good common sense" (*Messages of the First Presidency,* comp. James R. Clark [Salt Lake City: Bookcraft, 1970], 4:55–86).

President J. Reuben Clark gave this advice to help us determine if someone is speaking the mind and will of the Lord: "I have given some thought to this question, and the answer thereto so far as I can determine, is: We can tell when the speakers are 'moved upon by the Holy Ghost' only when we, ourselves, are 'moved upon by the Holy Ghost.' In a way, this completely shifts the responsibility from them to us to determine when they so speak" (*Church News,* July 31, 1954).

President Clark then quoted President Brigham Young, who said, "I am more afraid that this people have so much confidence in their leaders that they will not inquire for themselves of God whether they are led by Him. I am fearful they settle down in a state of blind self-security, trusting their eternal destiny in the hands of their leaders with a reckless confidence that in itself would thwart the purposes of God in their salvation, and weaken that influence they could give to their leaders, did they know for themselves, by the revelations of Jesus, that they are led in the right way. Let every man and woman know, by the whispering of the Spirit of God to themselves, whether their leaders are walking in the path the Lord dictates, or not" (*Journal of Discourses* 9:150).

This counsel from President Clark and President Young has been repeated in recent years by Ezra Taft Benson and Harold B. Lee, among others (see Conference Reports October 1963 and April 1970). Elder Benson summarized, "These then, are the three tests: The standard works; the inspired words of the Presidents of the Church, particularly the living Presidents; and the promptings of the Holy Ghost." We need to be responsible, to think, to prayerfully evaluate what we read, and to be careful about what we teach.

TIP: You can learn about a book's author on the Books tab of GospeLink Explorer (see page 122).

 CONTENTS

After considering the book's title page and author, look over its contents page. What do the chapter titles tell you about what you might expect to learn? What is the structure of the book? Is it divided into parts? What are the parts called, and how are they ordered? Can you tell from the contents page how the authors see their subject and what they are trying to accomplish?

NOTE: You can look at the contents of a book by expanding the Books window full screen and expanding the book and its chapters in the table of contents (see pages 40–42).

 PREFACE

Next, if the book has a preface or introduction, read it. Often, that is where authors will discuss their purpose in writing. For example, in the introduction to *Jesus the Christ*, Elder Talmage writes, "The purpose of the present treatise is that of considering the life and mission of Jesus *as* the Christ." He then goes on to discuss, as the contents page notes, the "scope and purpose" of the book from beginning to end.

After reading a book's preface or introduction, you might want to read here and there in the book, moving from chapter to chapter, just to get a general idea of the kinds of things the authors are talking about and the positions they take.

QUESTIONS

Finally, ask yourself some questions about the book:

What is the authors' purpose in writing the book? If you can put your finger on that, you'll be able to read the book with better understanding, and you'll be able to judge whether or not the authors met their goal.

Whom are the authors trying to reach? Sometimes the book will say this outright, but more often you'll have to dig for it. But if you know it, it will help you understand why the authors say what they do.

Once you've given a book this kind of overview, you'll be in a much better position to understand it than if you had just started reading. In fact, you may discover that the book isn't what you were looking for at all. You are then free to move on and not spend any more time on it. On the other hand, if the book *is* what you're looking for, you'll go on to read it faster and with better understanding—and that's the real point of surveying a book before you begin to read it.

READING A BOOK

Once you have a broad understanding of the book, you're ready to start reading in earnest. You've already read the preface or introduction, so go ahead and dive in to chapter 1. As you read, pay attention. Take notes with Composer or the Personal Notes view of the References window. Add your own comments with personal text notes. Use highlighting and bookmarks. Ask questions. Get involved! Reading shouldn't be a passive activity. It should be an active process of thinking and learning.

COMPARATIVE READING

As you read, you may find yourself wondering what other authors have said about a particular subject. With GospeLink, it's easy to find out, especially by using the Subject and Index tabs in GospeLink Explorer (see pages 133–36 and 137–41). When you start reading in this way, you've reached a new level of reading—one where you're not just trying to read what an author has to say but also learning what many authors have had to say on a certain subject. These different viewpoints will help lead you to new levels of understanding.

As you read, you may be surprised to find that authors sometimes disagree with each other on certain points about gospel topics, but this should not alarm you. The gospel is eternal, but our understanding of it is not. Also, remember that we are still learning— we believe in continuing revelation, and new understanding or practices or teachings may supersede those of earlier times.

Elder B. H. Roberts wrote, "The conditions under which the Church of Christ exists in various ages are constantly changing; and the officers of the church always require divine direction, which can only be supplied by revelation. The revelations given to the patriarchs from Adam to Abraham and Melchisedek were not esteemed sufficient to direct Moses in the management of the dispensation committed to him. Nor were the numerous revelations given to Moses sufficient to guide his successor, Joshua, in leading Israel; but a means for obtaining the word of the Lord was provided for him through the use of the Urim and Thummim, in the hands of the high priest. So also the revelations given to Moses, to Joshua and his successors, the judges and prophets of Israel, were not considered sufficient to direct the labors of the apostles and seventies and elders in the dispensation of the gospel introduced by the Lord Jesus. . . . In like manner, in all succeeding generations, and no less in our own than in any that has preceded it, the ministry of the Church of Christ stands absolutely in need of the spirit of prophecy and revelation to direct its labors, if those labors are to be efficient and acceptable to God" (*New Witnesses for God,* 1:150–52).

LEARNING MORE ABOUT READING

For more information on reading, studying, and learning, try doing the following with GospeLink:

 TO STUDY THE SCRIPTURES ABOUT READING:

1. Start GospeLink Explorer by clicking the **Explorer** button on the main toolbar.
2. Click the **Topics** tab.
3. Click the **R** alphabet button.
4. Click one of the topics under **Reading,** such as "Education" or "Study."

5. Study the scriptures displayed in the window on the right, taking notes about how you might apply what they have to say.

TO READ SOME OF THE BOOKS ABOUT LEARNING:

1. Start GospeLink Explorer by clicking the **Explorer** button on the main toolbar.
2. Click the **Subjects** tab.
3. Click the **S** alphabet button.
4. Click **Study, Learning.**
5. Click the title of a book that looks interesting.
6. Click the **Go To** button.

You can read the book, highlight meaningful passages, and apply suggestions and ideas.

TO USE THE COMPREHENSIVE INDEX TO LEARN MORE ABOUT READING:

1. Start GospeLink Explorer by clicking the **Explorer** button on the main toolbar.
2. Click the **Index** tab.
3. Type the word *reading* in the search box at the bottom of the screen.
4. Click the **Search** button.
5. Click the **R** alphabet button.
6. Click the right mouse button in the Comprehensive Index window on the left.
7. Click **Next Match.**
8. Repeat steps 6 and 7 until you see the topic *Reading.*
9. Click one of the book titles under the topic.

Now you can preview the book passage on that topic in the right window or click the **Go To** button to go to the passage in the book. As you go through several of these passages, you'll find a wealth of information to help you.

TIP: Use GospeLink to find information on related topics, such as intelligence, knowledge, study, wisdom, education, and so on.

CHAPTER 40
STUDYING THE SCRIPTURES

Even with the enormous number of books in GospeLink, your study of the gospel should start with the scriptures, continue with the scriptures, and end with the scriptures. They are at the heart of everything that has ever been said about the gospel. That is why GospeLink puts the scriptures into their own window on your screen. With GospeLink, studying the scriptures is easier than ever before.

There are a variety of ways to study the scriptures. For example, you could simply read them from beginning to end, which is certainly worth doing. But maybe you'd like to study a certain topic, such as prayer, service, or the atonement. Maybe you'd be interested in reading scripture stories to find principles you can apply in your own life. Perhaps you'd like to study the scriptures as history—or as literature, looking at poetry, sermons, language, structure, and so on. You might also study the comparisons and contrasts between various areas of the scriptures, such as the Old Testament and the New Testament, or between various people, such as Cain and Abel, or Sarai and Hagar. The scriptures are an endless source of insight, interest, and inspiration, and you should study them in a systematic way that is interesting and meaningful to you and that helps you to grow spiritually.

READING THE SCRIPTURES FROM BEGINNING TO END

One way to study the scriptures is to read them from beginning to end. This is the approach President Spencer W. Kimball took in reading the Bible as a fourteen-year-old boy. Here's what he said later about his experience:

"Let me tell you of one of the goals that I made when I was still but a lad. When I heard a Church leader from Salt Lake City tell us at conference that we should read the scriptures, and I recognized that I had never read the Bible, that very night at the conclusion of that very sermon I walked to my home a block away and climbed up in my little attic room in the top of the house and lighted a little coal-oil lamp that was on the little table, and I read the first chapters of Genesis. A year later I closed the Bible, having read every chapter in that big and glorious book.

"I found that this Bible that I was reading had in it 66 books, and then I was nearly dissuaded when I found that it had in it, 1,189 chapters, and then I also found that it had 1,519 pages. It was formidable, but I knew if others did it that I could do it.

"I found that there were certain parts that were hard for a 14-year-old boy to understand. There were some pages that were not especially interesting to me, but when I had read the 66 books and 1,189 chapters and 1,519 pages, I had a glowing satisfaction that I had made a goal and that I had achieved it.

"Now I am not telling you this story to boast; I am merely using this as an example to say that if I could do it by coal-oil light, you can do it by electric light. I have always been glad I read the Bible from cover to cover" ("Planning for a Full and Abundant Life," General Conference Priesthood Session, April 1974).

Sadly, many Latter-day Saints go through their whole lives without having read the standard works of the Church. If you haven't read them, why not make your purchase of GospeLink an excuse to immerse yourself in these wonderful books? As the Prophet Joseph Smith said of the Bible, "He who reads it oftenest will like it best" (*History of the Church* 2:14).

If you're interested in reading the scriptures through from beginning to end, you may want to read according to a set schedule—for example, so many verses or chapters each day. The main benefit in reading this way is that you'll get a broad overview of the scriptures in a reasonable amount of time—and that is well worth doing. Knowing this, some seminary classes have held Book of Mormon marathons where they read the entire Book of Mormon in twenty-four hours. Although that may be a bit extreme, reading the Book of Mormon in a fairly short time will help you understand its overall message as nothing else can.

Another way to read through the scriptures, however, is to read for a certain amount of time each day, with no concern about how far you get, just seeing how much you can learn and grow from the experience. This is one way of studying the scriptures in depth, and it is one of the best ways to study them.

PONDERING THE SCRIPTURES

The foundation of reading in-depth is pondering—taking time to think deeply about what you are reading and what you can learn from it. Pondering the scriptures will help open your mind to the power of the Holy Ghost, who is our true teacher. Consider these words of

Nephi: "I had desired to know the things that my father had seen, and believing that the Lord was able to make them known unto me, as I sat *pondering in mine heart* I was caught away in the Spirit of the Lord" (1 Nephi 11:1). Similarly, President Joseph F. Smith wrote at the beginning of his record of a vision, "I sat in my room *pondering over the scriptures*" (D&C 128:1). (For an interesting exercise, use GospeLink to see how many more examples you can find.)

Pondering brings the words of the scriptures to life. It lets the Holy Ghost use the word of the Lord to his children generally and apply it to you specifically to give you your own enlightenment and direction.

PAYING ATTENTION

Reading in depth also means paying attention to what seem to be little things but are actually big things, or to things you vaguely wonder about but haven't actually thought about or researched. You might liken this process to finding a loose bit of yarn on a sweater. It's easy to ignore that bit of yarn and just go on your way, but if you begin pulling on it, you may find it's the end of a very long thread with all kinds of interesting twists and turns.

Let's take an example from the scriptures—the very first verse of the Bible: "In the beginning, God created the heaven and the earth." It's easy to just read those familiar words and go on. But if you're paying attention, they may raise several questions in your mind, questions that might be worth considering. For example, what does the Bible mean by "the beginning"? The beginning of what? "God created." Who is God? Where did he come from? How did he create? And so on.

USING PERSONAL TEXT NOTES

As you think about such questions, you may think of possible answers, and you may also receive insights through the Spirit. If so, you may want to write them down in a personal text note, which will automatically stay with that scripture verse for future reference.

USING OTHER BOOKS AS COMMENTARY

You may want to see what General Authorities and gospel scholars have had to say about a verse you are reading. You can do this easily in GospeLink by clicking on the **Cross-References** button in the References window. Then, in the Books window, you'll see the text of other books in the library that comment on the verse. It's like being able to find that scripture reference in a whole library of books at one time, and it turns the entire library into an enormous commentary on the scriptures.

If you want, you can use this feature to see only what General Authorities have had to say about a scripture. To do so, click the **General Authorities** button at the bottom of the Books window.

Using the References Window

As you study, if there's a word or sentence you don't understand, don't just move on. Instead, take advantage of some of the works listed in the References window at the bottom of your screen. The References window offers a number of resources to help you better understand the scriptures, including *Webster's 1828 Dictionary, Strong's Greek Dictionary, Strong's Hebrew Dictionary, Smith's Bible Dictionary,* and *Easton's Bible Dictionary.*

Webster's 1828 Dictionary

Webster's 1828 *American Dictionary of the English Language* was published in America just one year before the Book of Mormon and thus reflects the language of Joseph Smith's time. For example, let's say you're reading D&C 121:43, which says, "Reproving betimes with sharpness, when moved upon by the Holy Ghost." There's that little word *betimes,* which you've read a hundred times. You've subconsciously assumed that it means "at times," but now, reading carefully and asking yourself questions, you wonder if that's right. If you double-click the word *betimes* and then look in *Webster's 1828 Dictionary* in the References window, you'll see the definition that Joseph Smith would have understood: "Seasonably; in good season or time; before it is late." So the point of the scripture is that we should not put off reproving someone when moved upon by the Holy Ghost to do so; we should follow the prompting, look for a good time to do it, and do it before it is too late. By understanding that one word, you've come to a better understanding of an important principle of the gospel.

Unlike Webster's 1806 dictionary, which is small and preliminary, Webster's 1828 dictionary is a major work, an American classic of hundreds of pages that includes many thousands of definitions and word etymologies.

Strong's Greek Dictionary and Strong's Hebrew Dictionary

Two other enlightening works in the References window are *Strong's Greek Dictionary* and *Strong's Hebrew Dictionary.* These dictionaries explain the meanings of the words from which the Bible was translated. Again, let's use Genesis 1:1 for an example: "In the beginning . . ." If you clicked on the word "beginning" and then looked in *Strong's Hebrew Dictionary* in the References window, you'd see the Hebrew word for "beginning," which is *rêshîyth*. You'd also see that the word means "The first, in place, time, order or rank."

Joseph Smith, when studying Hebrew, used this kind of information to explain, "An unlearned boy must give you a little Hebrew. *Berosheit* [there's our *rêshîyth*] *baurau, Eloheim ait aushamayeen vehau auraits*, rendered by King James' translators, 'In the beginning God created the heaven and the earth.' I want to analyze the word *Berosheit. Rosh*, the head [or "the first"]; *Sheit*, a grammatical termination; the *Baith* was not originally put there when the inspired man wrote it, but it has been since added. . . . *Baurau* signified to bring forth; *Eloheim* is from the word *Eloi, God,* in the singular number; and by adding the word *heim*, it renders it Gods. It read first, 'In the beginning the head of the Gods brought forth the Gods,' or, as others have translated it, 'The head of the Gods called the Gods together'" (*Discourses of the Prophet Joseph Smith,* pp. 36–37).

Joseph Smith got this kind of insight just from the first sentence of the Bible. For a fascinating exercise, try looking up every significant word in the first chapter of Genesis. You'll understand it as never before.

SMITH'S BIBLE DICTIONARY AND EASTON'S BIBLE DICTIONARY

Smith's Bible Dictionary and *Easton's Bible Dictionary* are two well known, nationally published Bible dictionaries. You can use them to look up all kinds of Bible-related topics. Their commentary on doctrinal and spiritual matters may or may not agree with LDS theology, but their explanations of biblical places, people, customs, plants, animals, and so on are extremely useful.

For example, let's say we wanted to know more about Paul's hometown of Tarsus. *Smith's Bible Dictionary* gives the following explanation: "Tarsus the chief town of Cilicia, 'no mean city' in other respects, but illustrious to all time as the birthplace and early residence of the apostle Paul. Acts 9:11; Acts 21:39; Acts 22:3. Even in the flourishing period of Greek history it was a city of some considerable consequence. In the civil wars of Rome it took Caesar's side . . ." and so on.

STUDYING THE SCRIPTURES BY TOPIC

You may be interested in reading scriptures about a particular topic, such as repentance or testimony. If so, you'll find Deseret Book's *Topical Guide to the Scriptures* an invaluable tool. This reference work, published in 1977, is the basis for the Topical Guide used in the scriptures published by the Church. You'll find it in GospeLink Explorer under the Topics tab. It lets you select a topic and then read all the scriptures associated with that topic. You could look up all these scriptures in your printed scriptures if you had many hours to spare. But GospeLink lets you look up these scriptures all at one time in a matter of seconds. Deseret Book's *Topical Guide* is also a great tool if you need to prepare a lesson or talk on a particular topic. For instructions on how to use it, see the chapter on Topic Explorer on pages 115–17.

LEARNING MORE ABOUT STUDYING THE SCRIPTURES

For additional information on studying the scriptures, try doing the following with GospeLink:

 TO READ SOME OF THE BOOKS ABOUT SCRIPTURE STUDY:

1. Start GospeLink Explorer by clicking the **Explorer** button on the main toolbar.
2. Click the **Subjects** tab.
3. Click the **S** alphabet button.
4. Click **Scripture** or **Scripture Commentary.**
5. Click the title of a book that looks interesting.
6. Click the **Go To** button.

You can read the book, highlight meaningful passages, and think of ways to apply what you learn to your own scripture study. The following are books in GospeLink that you might find useful in learning more about how to study the scriptures:

Marking the Scriptures, by Daniel H. Ludlow
Raising Up a Family to the Lord, by Gene R. Cook
The Power of the Word, by Robert L. Millet
You, Your Family, and the Scriptures, by Ed J. Pinegar
Feasting upon the Word, by Dennis and Sandra Packard

TO STUDY THE SCRIPTURES ABOUT SCRIPTURE STUDY:

1. Start GospeLink Explorer by clicking the **Explorer** button on the main toolbar.

2. Click the **Topics** tab.

3. Click the **S** alphabet button.

4. Click one of the topics under **Scriptures, Study.**

5. Study the scriptures displayed in the window on the right.

 TO USE THE COMPREHENSIVE INDEX TO LEARN MORE ABOUT SCRIPTURE STUDY:

1. Start GospeLink Explorer by clicking the **Explorer** button on the main toolbar.

2. Click the **Index** tab.

3. Type the words *scripture study* in the search box at the bottom of the screen.

4. Click the **Search** button.

5. Click the **S** alphabet button.

6. Click the right mouse button in the Comprehensive Index window on the left.

7. Click **Next Match.**

8. Repeat steps 6 and 7 until you see the long list of topics that begins with the words *Scripture Study.*

9. Browse through the topics until you see one that looks interesting.

10. Click one of the book titles under the topic.

Now you can preview the book passage on that topic in the right window or click the **Go To** button to go to the passage in the book.

CHAPTER 41

BECOMING A GOSPEL SCHOLAR

What does it mean to be a gospel scholar? Well, what does it mean to you?

Does it mean you can quote important scriptures by chapter and verse?

Does it mean you've studied the scriptures deeply?

Does it mean you've studied the words of the prophets, both ancient and modern?

Does it mean you have a broad overview of LDS literature?

Does it mean you've carefully studied the classics of LDS literature?

Does it mean all of the above?

Or does it mean something more? This chapter includes some ideas on what it might mean to be a gospel scholar.

A GENERAL ACQUAINTANCE WITH LDS LITERATURE

At its most superficial level, being a gospel scholar might mean being generally acquainted with the classics of LDS literature—the scriptures themselves and such books as *Jesus the Christ* and *The Articles of Faith*, by James E. Talmage. This, however, is only the beginning. Classic American writer Washington Irving described this basic level of scholarship in this way: "Writers will write, printers will print, and the world will inevitably be overstocked with good books. It will soon be the employment of a lifetime merely to learn their names. Many a man of passable information, at the present day, reads scarcely any thing but reviews; and before long a man of erudition will be little better than a mere walking catalogue" ("The Mutability of Literature," in *The Sketch Book*).

This is a beginning, but we must do better.

A DEEP ACQUAINTANCE WITH LDS LITERATURE

To attain any real level of scholarship, we must actually *read* the books we so glibly mention in our conversations with others as if we knew something about them. That requires time and thought and effort, but there is no other way. As Euclid said to the king who wondered if there weren't some shortcut, "Your Highness, there is no royal road to geometry."

"What about learning by the Spirit?" some may ask. "Isn't that a 'royal road' to learning?" Yes, but even for that, effort is required—not because the Lord wants to make things difficult but because without sowing there can be no harvest. That's just the way things are. As the Lord told Oliver Cowdery, "Behold, you have not understood; you have supposed that I would give it unto you, when you took no thought save it was to ask me. But, behold, I say unto you, that you must study it out in your mind" (D&C 9:7–8). And Joseph Smith said, "The things of God are of deep import; and time, and experience, and careful and ponderous and solemn thoughts can only find them out" (*History of the Church* 3:295).

SPIRITUAL KNOWLEDGE

Nevertheless, spiritual knowledge is available to those who seek it and live for it. As the Lord told Joseph Smith, "Let thy bowels . . . be full of charity towards all men, and to the household of faith, and let virtue garnish thy thoughts unceasingly; then shall thy confidence wax strong in the presence of God; and *the doctrine of the priesthood shall distil upon thy soul as the dews from heaven. The Holy Ghost shall be thy constant companion,* and thy scepter an unchanging scepter of righteousness and truth; and thy dominion shall be an everlasting dominion, and without compulsory means it shall flow unto thee forever and ever" (D&C 121:45–46; italics added).

"The Spirit of Revelation is in connection with these blessings," the Prophet said. "A person may profit by noticing the first intimation of the spirit of revelation; for instance, when you feel pure intelligence flowing into you, it may give you sudden strokes of ideas. . . .Thus, by learning the Spirit of God and understanding it, you may grow into the principle of revelation" (*History of the Church* 3:381).

He also noted, speaking from experience, "Could you gaze into heaven five minutes, you would know more than you would by reading all that ever was written on the subject. . . . Truth . . . can and may be known through the revelations of God in the way of His ordinances, and in answer to prayer" (*History of the Church* 6:50–51).

GOODNESS AND HUMILITY

As important as such knowledge is, it is as nothing when compared with the need to actually *live* the gospel. That is what Paul meant when he said, "Though I have the gift of prophecy, and understand all mysteries, and all knowledge; and though I have all faith, so that I could remove mountains, and have not charity, I am nothing" (1 Corinthians 13:2).

Thomas à Kempis, who lived from 1379 to 1471, was an Augustinian monk who spent his entire life in poverty and obscurity. Nevertheless, his book *The Imitation of Christ* has lived through the centuries as a classic of inspirational literature. In it he wrote:

"Every man naturally desires knowledge; but what good is knowledge without fear of God? Indeed a humble rustic who serves God is better than a proud intellectual who neglects his soul. . . .

". . . Intellectuals like to appear learned and to be called wise. Yet there are many things the knowledge of which does little or no good to the soul. . . .

"The more you know and the better you understand, the more severely will you be judged, unless your life is also the more holy. Do not be proud, therefore, because of your learning or skill. Rather, fear because of the talent given you. If you think you know many things and understand them well enough, realize at the same time that there is much you do not know. Hence, do not affect wisdom, but admit your ignorance. Why prefer yourself to anyone else when many are more learned, more cultured than you? . . .

"What, therefore, have we to do with questions of philosophy? He to whom the Eternal Word [God] speaks is free from theorizing. For from this Word are all things, and of Him all things speak—the Beginning Who also speaks to us. Without this Word no man understands or judges aright. He to whom it becomes everything, who traces all things to it and who sees all things in it, may ease his heart and remain at peace with God."

Notice that Thomas is not saying "Don't learn and study." He is saying that learning is something more than being a "proud intellectual," that knowledge creates obligation, that without humility and goodness knowledge is worthless, and that true knowledge has nothing to do with "questions of philosophy" but comes from God. Thomas knew something about what it means to be a gospel scholar.

CONTINUAL LEARNING AND EXPANSION

Ultimately, the gospel includes everything that is "virtuous, lovely, or of good report or praiseworthy" (Articles of Faith 1:13). Brigham Young once said, "'Shall I sit down and read the Bible, the Book of Mormon, and the Book of Covenants all the time?' says one. Yes, if you please, and when you have done, you may be nothing but a sectarian after all. It is your duty to study . . . everything upon the face of the earth, in addition to reading those books" (*Discourses of Brigham Young*, 256).

He also noted, "Let us not narrow ourselves up; for the world, with all its variety of useful information and its rich hoard of hidden treasure, is before us; and eternity, with all its sparkling intelligence, lofty aspirations, and unspeakable glories, is before us" (*Discourses of Brigham Young*, 279).

"Thy mind, O man!" said Joseph Smith, "if thou wilt lead a soul to salvation, must stretch as high as the utmost heavens, and search into and contemplate the darkest abyss, and the broad expanse of eternity" (*History of the Church* 3:295).

Learning should be a lifetime endeavor—and that is just the beginning! As Brigham Young said, "When shall we cease to learn? I will give you my opinion about it: never, never" (*Discourses of Brigham Young*, 249).

As you continue in your quest for knowledge of all that is good and true and beautiful, we wish you the best, and we hope you will find GospeLink useful in your study of the gospel and all it comprises.

LEARNING MORE ABOUT GOSPEL SCHOLARSHIP

For additional information on gospel scholarship, try doing the following with GospeLink:

 TO READ SOME OF THE BOOKS ABOUT WISDOM AND KNOWLEDGE:

1. Start GospeLink Explorer by clicking the **Explorer** button on the main toolbar.
2. Click the **Subjects** tab.
3. Click the **K** alphabet button.
4. Click **Knowledge.**
5. Click the title of a book that looks interesting.
6. Click the **Go To** button.

7. Repeat the steps above for **Wisdom.**

You can read the books, highlight meaningful passages, and so on. Here are some of the books you might find useful:

Expressions of Faith, edited by Susan Easton Black

In Search of Truth, by John A. Widtsoe

Nibley on the Timely and the Timeless, by Hugh Nibley

The World and the Prophets, by Hugh Nibley

 TO STUDY THE SCRIPTURES ABOUT WISDOM AND KNOWLEDGE:

1. Start GospeLink Explorer by clicking the **Explorer** button on the main toolbar.

2. Click the **Topics** tab.

3. Click the **W** alphabet button.

4. Click one of the topics under **Wisdom.**

5. Study the scriptures displayed in the window on the right.

6. Repeat the steps above for **Knowledge.**

 TO USE THE COMPREHENSIVE INDEX TO LEARN MORE ABOUT GOSPEL SCHOLARSHIP:

1. Start GospeLink Explorer by clicking the **Explorer** button on the main toolbar.

2. Click the **Index** tab.

3. Type the word *scholarship* in the search box at the bottom of the screen.

4. Click the **Search** button.

5. Click the **S** alphabet button.

6. Click the right mouse button in the Comprehensive Index window on the left.

7. Click **Next Match.**

8. Repeat steps 6 and 7 until you see the long list of topics that begins with the word *Scholarship.*

9. Browse through the topics until you see one that looks interesting.

10. Click one of the book titles under the topic.

Now you can preview the book passage on that topic in the right window or click the **Go To** button to go to the passage in the book.

TIP: Use GospeLink to find information on related topics, such as learning, study, education, spirituality, goodness, and so on.

APPENDIX 1
GOSPEL STUDY GUIDE

This study guide doesn't begin to include all of the books in GospeLink, but it does list some that we have found especially useful and informative, or that have been influential or historically important. Many of them might be considered classics. To find these books, use the Books tab in GospeLink Explorer (see pages 118–24). To find other books on various subjects, use the Subjects tab in GospeLink Explorer (see pages 133–36).

APOLOGETICS

NOTE: Apologetic works are works that defend the Church.

Abraham in Egypt
Ancient American Setting for the Book of Mormon
Approach to the Book of Mormon
Defense of the Faith and the Saints
Investigating the Book of Mormon Witnesses
Key to Theology
Lehi in the Desert/The World of the Jaredites/There Were Jaredites
Marvelous Work and a Wonder
Mormonism and Early Christianity
New Witness for Christ in America
New Witnesses for God
Our Search for Happiness: An Invitation to Understand The Church of Jesus Christ of Latter-day Saints
Rational Theology
Rediscovering the Book of Mormon
Reinvestigating the Book of Mormon
Since Cumorah
Voice of Warning

DOCTRINES OF THE GOSPEL

Articles of Faith
Discourses of Brigham Young
Discourses of Joseph Smith
Doctrines of the Kingdom
God, Man, and the Universe
Gospel and Man's Relationship to Deity
Gospel Doctrine
Gospel Standards
Gospel Truth
Jesus Christ, Key to the Plan of Salvation
Key to the Science of Theology
Lectures on Faith
Mediation and Atonement
Mormon Doctrine of Deity
Our Father's Plan
Our Search for Happiness
Principles and Practices of the Restored Gospel
Prophets, Priesthood Keys, and Succession
Teachings of the Prophet Joseph Smith

GENERAL BIOGRAPHY

Autobiography of Philo Dibble (in *Early Scenes from Church History*)
Autobiography of Parley P. Pratt
Camilla, a Biography of Camilla Eyring Kimball
Henry Ballard: The Story of a Courageous Pioneer, 1832–1908
Hyrum Smith, Patriarch
In the Gospel Net
J. Golden Kimball: The Story of a Unique Personality
Jacob Hamblin: A Narrative of His Personal Experience
Life of David W. Patten, the First Apostolic Martyr
Life of Heber C. Kimball
Mary Fielding Smith, Daughter of Britain: Portrait of Courage
Mothers of the Prophets
My Life's Review
Prisoner for Conscience' Sake: The Life of George Reynolds
Sermons and Missionary Services of Melvin J. Ballard
Stalwarts of Mormonism
Supporting Saints
They Knew the Prophet

William Clayton's Journal: A Daily Record of the Journey of the
    Original Company of "Mormon" Pioneers from Nauvoo, Illinois,
    to the Valley of the Great Salt Lake
Women of Mormondom

GOSPEL LIVING

All These Things Shall Give Thee Experience
Believing Christ
Broken Heart
Counseling with Our Councils: Learning to Minister Together in the
    Church and in the Family
Faith Precedes the Miracle
Faith: The Essence of True Religion
Feed My Sheep: Leadership Ideas for Latter-day Shepherds
Gospel Ideals
Holiness of Everyday Life
Legacies of Jesus
Living by the Power of Faith
Lord's Way
More Excellent Way: Essays on Leadership for Latter-day Saints
Our Search for Happiness
Principles and Practices of the Restored Gospel
Receiving Answers to Our Prayers
Seek Ye Diligently
Simeon Solution: One Woman's Spiritual Odyssey

HISTORY OF THE CHURCH

Century of Mormonism in Great Britain
Colonia Juarez: An Intimate Account of a Mormon Village
Comprehensive History of The Church of Jesus Christ of Latter-day
    Saints
Dawning of a Brighter Day
Essentials in Church History
Eyewitness Accounts of the Restoration
Far West Record: Minutes of the Church of Jesus Christ of Latter-day
    Saints, 1830–1844
Heavens Resound: A History of the Latter-day Saints in Ohio, 1830–
    1838
History of The Church of Jesus Christ of Latter-day Saints
In Old Nauvoo: Everyday Life in the City of Joseph
Joseph Smith's Kirtland

Men with a Mission, 1837–1841: The Quorum of the Twelve Apostles in the British Isles
Missouri Persecutions
Mormon Battalion: Its History and Achievements
Restored Church
Rise and Fall of Nauvoo
Story of the Latter-day Saints
Women of Covenant
Women's Voices: An Untold History of the Latter-day Saints, 1830–1900

PIONEERS

Fragments of Experience
Growing Up in Zion
I Walked to Zion
Journey to Zion
Mary Fielding Smith, Daughter of Britain
Pioneer Stories
String of Pearls
William Clayton's Journal

LIVES OF THE PROPHETS

JOSEPH SMITH

History of Joseph Smith by His Mother
Joseph Smith, an American Prophet
Joseph Smith, the Man and the Seer
Life of Joseph the Prophet
Personal Writings of Joseph Smith
They Knew the Prophet

BRIGHAM YOUNG

Brigham Young at Home
Brigham Young, the Man and His Work
Life Story of Brigham Young
Lion of the Lord: Essays on the Life and Service of Brigham Young
Manuscript History of Brigham Young

JOHN TAYLOR

Life of John Taylor

WILFORD WOODRUFF
Leaves from My Journal
Wilford Woodruff, His Life and Labors

LORENZO SNOW
Biography and Family Record of Lorenzo Snow

JOSEPH F. SMITH
Life of Joseph F. Smith

HEBER J. GRANT
Heber J. Grant: Highlights in the Life of a Great Leader

GEORGE ALBERT SMITH
See individual chapters in:
Dynamic Disciples, Prophets of God
In the Company of Prophets
Presidents of the Church

DAVID O. MCKAY
Cherished Experiences from the Writings of President David O.
*   McKay*
Highlights in the Life of President David O. McKay
Home Memories of President David O. McKay

JOSEPH FIELDING SMITH
Joseph Fielding Smith: Gospel Scholar, Prophet of God
Life of Joseph Fielding Smith

HAROLD B. LEE
Harold B. Lee: Man of Vision, Prophet of God

SPENCER W. KIMBALL
Spencer W. Kimball: Resolute Disciple, Prophet of God

EZRA TAFT BENSON
Ezra Taft Benson

HOWARD W. HUNTER
Howard W. Hunter

GORDON B. HINCKLEY
Go Forward with Faith: The Biography of Gordon B. Hinckley

MARRIAGE AND FAMILY

Are My Children Going to Make It? Real Help for Teaching the
    Gospel in the Home
Bringing Up Moral Children
Dealing with Differences in Marriage
Families Are Forever . . . If I Can Just Get through Today!
Families Who Laugh . . . Last
Foundations for a Happier Marriage
Helping Your Children Stay Morally Clean
Just for Newlyweds
Marriage and Divorce: An Address
Marriage Talk: How to Communicate with Your Spouse
One Flesh, One Heart: Putting Celestial Love into Your Temple
    Marriage
Raising Up a Family to the Lord
That My Family Should Partake
Twelve Traps in Today's Marriage and How to Avoid Them
What Happy Families Are Doing
What Husbands Expect of Wives
What Wives Expect of Husbands
When a Child Wanders
You, Your Family and the Scriptures

MISSIONARY WORK

Dawning of a Brighter Day: The Church in Black Africa
Home with Honor: Helps for Returning Missionaries
Making Your Home a Missionary Training Center
Missionary Experiences
Morning Breaks: Stories of Conversion and Faith in the Former Soviet
    Union
Prepare with Honor: Helps for Future Missionaries
Serve with Honor: Helps for Missionaries
Sharing the Gospel with Others
We'll Bring the World His Truth: Missionary Adventures from
    Around the World

SELF-HELP AND INSPIRATION

Breaking the Cycle of Compulsive Behavior
Counseling: A Guide to Helping Others

Divine Connection: Understanding Your Inherent Worth
Doing the Right Things for the Right Reasons
Finding Light in a Dark World
Finding Peace in Our Lives
Finding Peace in Troubled Waters: Ten Life Preservers for When
  Your Ship Springs a Leak
How to Succeed with People
However Long and Hard the Road
In the Strength of the Lord I Can Do All Things
Joy of the Journey
Overcoming Depression
Overcoming Personal Loss
Perfect Brightness of Hope
Spiritual Roots of Human Relations
Spirituality and Self-Esteem: Developing the Inner Self
When Drugs Hit Home
Wherefore, Ye Must Press Forward
Willpower Is Not Enough: Why We Don't Succeed at Change
Within Reach

STUDYING THE SCRIPTURES

Ancient Apostles
Book of Mormon Commentary (7 vols.)
Church of the Old Testament
Commentary on the Pearl of Great Price
Companion to Your Study of the Book of Mormon
Companion to Your Study of the Doctrine and Covenants, Vol. 1
Companion to Your Study of the Doctrine and Covenants, Vol. 2
Companion to Your Study of the New Testament: The Four Gospels
Companion to Your Study of the Old Testament
Doctrinal Commentary on the Pearl of Great Price
Doctrine and Covenants Commentary
Feasting Upon the Word
Isaiah, Plain and Simple
Isaiah: Prophet, Seer, and Poet
Jesus the Christ
Joseph Smith's Commentary on the Bible
Latter-day Prophets and the Doctrine and Covenants
Marking the Scriptures
Opening the Seven Seals: The Visions of John the Revelator
Power of the Word

*Revelations of the Prophet Joseph Smith: A Historical and
    Biographical Commentary of the Doctrine and Covenants*
Sacred Truths from the Doctrine and Covenants
Studies in Scripture, Vol. 1: The Doctrine and Covenants
Studies in Scripture, Vol. 2: The Pearl of Great Price
Studies in Scripture, Vol. 3: Genesis to 2 Samuel
Studies in Scripture, Vol. 4: 1 Kings to Malachi
Studies in Scripture, Vol. 5: The Gospels
Studies in Scripture, Vol. 6: Acts to Revelation
Studies in Scripture, Vol. 7: 1 Nephi to Alma 29
Studies in Scripture, Vol. 8: Alma 30 to Moroni
Teachings of the Doctrine and Covenants
Understanding Paul
Unknown Testament
Unlocking the Old Testament
Why the King James Version

UNDERSTANDING THE TEMPLE

House of Glory
House of the Lord
Temple and Cosmos: Beyond This Ignorant Present
Temple in Antiquity
Temples of the Ancient World

WOMEN'S INTERESTS

*As Women of Faith: Talks Selected from the BYU Women's
    Conferences*
Celebration! Ten Principles of More Joyous Living
Hearts Knit Together: Talks from the 1995 Women's Conference
I'm a Day Late and a Dollar Short . . . and It's Okay!
Lighten Up!
Love Is a Verb
My Beloved Sisters
My Neighbor, My Sister, My Friend
Needles in the Basket: Looking at Patterns of a Woman's Life
Our Sisters in the Bible
Our Sisters in the Latter-day Scriptures
Remarkable Stories from the Lives of Latter-day Saint Women, Vol. 1
Remarkable Stories from the Lives of Latter-day Saint Women, Vol. 2
Thoughts of a Grasshopper: Essays and Oddities

Woman and the Priesthood
Women and Christ: Living the Abundant Life
Women and the Power Within: To See Life Steadily and See It Whole
Women of Covenant: The Story of Relief Society
Women of Mormondom
Wondrous Power of a Mother

WORDS OF THE PROPHETS

NOTE: You can find many other words of the prophets in the form of discourses by using the Talks and Speakers tabs in GospeLink Explorer.

JOSEPH SMITH
Discourses of the Prophet Joseph Smith
Lectures on Faith: Delivered to the School of the Prophets in Kirtland, Ohio, 1834–35
Personal Writings of Joseph Smith
Teachings of the Prophet Joseph Smith
Words of Joseph Smith: The Contemporary Accounts of the Nauvoo Discourses of the Prophet Joseph

BRIGHAM YOUNG
Discourses of Brigham Young
Letters of Brigham Young to His Sons

JOHN TAYLOR
Gospel Kingdom: Selections from the Writings and Discourses of John Taylor, Third President of The Church of Jesus Christ of Latter-day Saints
Government of God
Mediation and Atonement

WILFORD WOODRUFF
Leaves from My Journal

LORENZO SNOW
Italian Mission

JOSEPH F. SMITH

From Prophet to Son: Advice of Joseph F. Smith to His Missionary Sons

Gospel Doctrine: Selections from the Sermons and Writings of Joseph F. Smith

HEBER J. GRANT

Gospel Standards: Selections from the Sermons and Writings of Heber J. Grant

GEORGE ALBERT SMITH

Sharing the Gospel with Others

DAVID O. MCKAY

Ancient Apostles

Cherished Experiences from the Writings of President David O. McKay

Gospel Ideals: Selections from the Discourses of David O. McKay

Home Memories of President David O. McKay

Man May Know for Himself: Teachings of President David O. McKay

JOSEPH FIELDING SMITH

Answers to Gospel Questions

Church History and Modern Revelation

Elijah the Prophet and His Mission

Essentials in Church History

Man, His Origin and Destiny

Origin of the Reorganized Church

Progress of Man

Restoration of All Things

Seek Ye Earnestly

Signs of the Times

Take Heed to Yourselves

Way to Perfection

HAROLD B. LEE

Decisions for Successful Living

Stand Ye in Holy Places

SPENCER W. KIMBALL
Faith Precedes the Miracle
Marriage and Divorce: An Address
My Beloved Sisters
President Kimball Speaks Out

EZRA TAFT BENSON
Come, Listen to a Prophet's Voice
Come unto Christ
So Shall Ye Reap
This Nation Shall Endure
Witness and a Warning: A Modern-Day Prophet Testifies of the Book of Mormon

HOWARD W. HUNTER
That We Might Have Joy

GORDON B. HINCKLEY
Be Thou an Example
Faith: The Essence of True Religion
Teachings of Gordon B. Hinckley

YOUTH
Decisions for Successful Living
Fragments of Experience
Gems for the Young Folks
Great Stories from Mormon History
I Walk by Faith
Joy of the Journey
My First Mission
String of Pearls
Walk Tall, You're a Daughter of God
What I Wish I'd Known in High School: A Crash Course in Teenage Survival
What I Wish I'd Known in High School: The Second Semester
Why Say No When the World Says Yes? Resisting Temptation in an Immoral World

APPENDIX 2
WHAT'S IN GOSPELINK

The list below reflects the latest information available about the contents of GospeLink. However, it may be incomplete and is subject to change.

SCRIPTURES

NOTE: Except for the 1830 edition of the Book of Mormon, the scriptures are available in the Scriptures window. (Click the Joseph Smith Translation button for the JST and the Standard Works button for everything else.)

Holy Bible (King James Version)
Book of Mormon
Doctrine and Covenants
Pearl of Great Price
Book of Mormon, 1830 edition (available in the Books window under Other LDS Authors).
Holy Scriptures—Inspired Version (the complete Joseph Smith Translation)

REFERENCE WORKS

NOTE: The reference works are available in the References window when using Disk A or Disk B. (Click the Virtual Encyclopedia button for the Virtual Encyclopedia and the Dictionaries button for the other reference works.)

Dictionary of the Book of Mormon, George Reynolds
Easton's Bible Dictionary
LDS Virtual Encyclopedia
Strong's Greek Dictionary
Strong's Hebrew Dictionary
Smith's Bible Dictionary

Topical Guide to the Scriptures (1977)
Webster's 1828 American Dictionary of the English Language

LDS PERIODICALS

NOTE: Except for the Index to the Ensign, the LDS periodicals are available in the Books window when using Disk B. (For the periodicals, click the Periodicals button. For the Index to the Ensign, click the Ensign Index button on the main toolbar.)

Conference Reports (144 issues)
Contributor (156 issues)
Elder's Journal (4 issues)
Evening and the Morning Star (24 issues)
Improvement Era (695 issues)
Index to the Ensign
Journal of Discourses (26 vols.)
Messenger and Advocate (36 issues)
Times and Seasons (132 issues)

GOSPEL CLASSICS, OLD AND NEW

NOTE: The gospel classics are available in the Books window when using Disk A. (Click the General Authorities button or the Other LDS Authors button.)

Aaronic Priesthood, Oscar W. McConkie
Abraham in Egypt, Hugh Nibley
Alive in Christ, Robert L. Millet
All Alone: Surviving the Loss of Your Spouse, Kathleen Rawlings Buntin
All These Things Shall Give Thee Experience, Neal A. Maxwell
Allegory of the Olive Tree, Stephen D. Ricks and John W. Welch, eds.
Alma, the Testimony of the Word, Monte S. Nyman and Charles D. Tate, Jr., eds.
Aloha! Chieko N. Okazaki
American Religions and the Rise of Mormonism, Milton V. Backman, Jr.
Ancient American Setting for the Book of Mormon, John L. Sorenson
Ancient Apostles, David O. McKay
Ancient State, Hugh Nibley
And They Came to Pass, Lee Benson
Angels, Oscar W. McConkie

Answers to Gospel Questions (5 vols.), Joseph Fielding Smith

Answers to Your Questions about the Doctrine and Covenants, Richard O. Cowan

Anticipations of the Civil War in Mormon Thought, Hyrum L. Andrus

Apocryphal Writings and the Latter-day Saints, C. Wilfred Griggs, ed.

Apostle Paul, His Life and His Testimony

Approach to the Book of Mormon, Hugh Nibley

Approaching Zion, Hugh Nibley

Archaeology and the Book of Mormon, Milton R. Hunter

Are My Children Going to Make It? R. Wayne Boss and Leslee S. Boss

Articles of Faith, James E. Talmage

As Women of Faith, Mary E. Stovall and Carol Cornwall Madsen, eds.

Autobiography of Parley P. Pratt, Parley P. Pratt

Be of Good Cheer, Marvin J. Ashton

Be Thou an Example, Gordon B. Hinckley

Behold the Lamb of God, J. Reuben Clark, Jr.

Behold, I Come Quickly, Hoyt W. Brewster, Jr.

Believing Christ, Stephen E. Robinson

Believing Heart, Bruce C. Hafen

Belonging Heart, Bruce C. Hafen and Marie K. Hafen

Best of Lowell L. Bennion, Lowell L. Bennion

Best-Loved Poems of the LDS People, Jack M. Lyon et al., eds.

Best-Loved Stories of the LDS People, Jack M. Lyon, Linda Ririe Gundry, and Jay A. Parry, eds.

Biography and Family Record of Lorenzo Snow, Eliza R. Snow

Blessed by the Hymns, LaVonne VanOrden, comp.

Book of John Whitmer, John Whitmer

Book of Mormon Authorship, Noel B. Reynolds, ed.

Book of Mormon: The Keystone Scripture, Paul R. Cheesman, ed.

Born That Way? Erin Eldridge

Breaking the Cycle of Compulsive Behavior, Martha Nibley Beck and John C. Beck

Brigham Young at Home, Clarissa Young Spencer with Mabel Harmer

Brigham Young: The Man and His Work, Preston Nibley

Bringing Up Moral Children, A. Lynn Scoresby

Broken Heart, Bruce C. Hafen

Brother Brigham Challenges the Saints, Hugh Nibley

By Study and Also by Faith (2 vols.), John M. Lundquist and Stephen D. Ricks, eds.

Call of Zion, Ronald D. Dennis

Camilla, a Biography of Camilla Eyring Kimball, Caroline Eyring Miner and Edward L. Kimball

Celebration of Christmas

Celebration! Ten Principles of More Joyous Living, Jaroldeen Asplund Edwards

Century of "Mormonism" in Great Britain, Richard L. Evans

Chainbreakers, Michele R. Sorensen

Cherished Experiences from the Writings of President David O. McKay, David O. McKay

Christ and the New Covenant, Jeffrey R. Holland

Christ in Ancient America, Milton R. Hunter

Christ the Son—Our God and Father, Hyrum L. Andrus

Christopher Columbus: A Latter-day Perspective, Arnold K. Garr

Church Chronology, Andrew Jenson

Church History and Modern Revelation (4 vols.), Joseph Fielding Smith

Church in War and Peace, Stephen L Richards

Church of the Old Testament, John A. Tvedtnes

Classic Stories from the Lives of Our Prophets, Leon R. Hartshorn, comp.

Colonia Juarez, Nelle Hatch

Come unto Christ, Ezra Taft Benson

Come, Listen to a Prophet's Voice, Ezra Taft Benson

Commentary on the Book of Mormon (7 vols.), George Reynolds and Janne M. Sjodahl

Commentary on the Pearl of Great Price, George Reynolds and Janne M. Sjodahl

Companion to Your Study of the Book of Mormon, Daniel H. Ludlow

Companion to Your Study of the Doctrine and Covenants (2 vols.), Daniel H. Ludlow

Companion to Your Study of the New Testament: The Four Gospels, Daniel H. Ludlow

Companion to Your Study of the Old Testament, Daniel H. Ludlow

Compendium of the Doctrines of the Gospel, Franklin D. Richards and James A. Little

Comprehensive History of The Church of Jesus Christ of Latter-day Saints (6 vols.), B. H. Roberts

Constitution, a Heavenly Banner, Ezra Taft Benson

Continuing the Quest, Hugh B. Brown

Converted to Christ through the Book of Mormon, Eugene England, ed.

Counseling (2 vols.), R. Lanier Britsch and Terrance D. Olson, eds.

Counseling with Our Councils, M. Russell Ballard

Creation, Frank B. Salisbury

Dawning of a Brighter Day, Alexander B. Morrison

Dead Sea Scrolls and Original Christianity, O. Preston Robinson

Dealing with Differences in Marriage, Brent A. Barlow

Decisions for Successful Living, Harold B. Lee

Defense of the Faith and the Saints (2 vols.), B. H. Roberts

Deity and Death, Spencer J. Palmer, ed.

Deposition of a Disciple, Neal A. Maxwell

Discourses of Brigham Young, Brigham Young; John A. Widtsoe, ed.

Discourses of the Prophet Joseph Smith, Joseph Smith; comp. Alma P. Burton

Distinct Doctrines and Teachings of the Pearl of Great Price, Hyrum L. Andrus

Divine Connection, Lloyd D. Newell

Divine Patriarchal Order, Hyrum L. Andrus

Doctrinal Commentary on the Pearl of Great Price, Hyrum L. Andrus

Doctrinal Themes of the Doctrine and Covenants, Hyrum L. Andrus

Doctrine and Covenants and the Future, Roy W. Doxey

Doctrine and Covenants Commentary, Hyrum M. Smith and Janne M. Sjodahl

Doctrine and Covenants Speaks (2 vols.), Roy W. Doxey

Doctrine and Covenants, a Book of Answers, Leon R. Hartshorn, Dennis A. Wright, and Craig J. Ostler, eds.

Doctrines for Exaltation

Doctrines of the Kingdom, Hyrum L. Andrus

Doing the Right Things for the Right Reasons, Richard L. Bednar and Scott R. Peterson

Doughnuts, Letters, and Midnight Phone Calls, Annette Paxman Bowen

Dynamic Disciples, Prophets of God, Francis M. Gibbons

Early Scenes in Church History

Effective Mormon Families, William G. Dyer and Phillip R. Kunz

Elect Ladies, Janet Peterson and LaRene Gaunt

Elias: An Epic of the Ages, Orson F. Whitney

Elijah the Prophet and His Mission, Joseph Fielding Smith

Encircled by Love, Jill C. Major, Lauren C. Leifson, Hollie C. Bevan

Enoch the Prophet, Hugh Nibley
Essentials in Church History, Joseph Fielding Smith
Eternal Love, Boyd K. Packer
Eternal Man, Truman G. Madsen
Even As I Am, Neal A. Maxwell
Evidences and Reconciliations, John A. Widtsoe
Exceptional Stories from the Lives of Our Apostles, Leon R.
     Hartshorn, comp.
Expressions of Faith, Susan Easton Black, ed.
Eye Single to the Glory of God, Robert L. Millet
Eye to Eye, Heart to Heart, Elaine L. Jack
Eyewitness Accounts of the Restoration, Milton V. Backman, Jr.
Ezra Taft Benson, Sheri L. Dew
Ezra Taft Benson Remembers the Joy of Christmas, Ezra Taft Benson
Faith, various General Authorities
Faith Precedes the Miracle, Spencer W. Kimball
Faith: The Essence of True Religion, Gordon B. Hinckley
Falling Away, B. H. Roberts
Families Are Forever . . . If I Can Just Get through Today! Janice
     Madsen Weinheimer
Families Who Laugh . . . Last, Janene Wolsey Baadsgaard
Family Finances for the Flabbergasted, Janene Wolsey Baadsgaard
Family Pecan Trees, Carlos E. Asay
Far West Record, Donald Q. Cannon and Lyndon W. Cook, eds.
Feasting upon the Word, Dennis and Sandra Packard
Feed My Sheep, Alexander B. Morrison
Finding a Friend in the Mirror, Shane R. Barker
Finding Light in a Dark World, James E. Faust
Finding Peace in Our Lives, Joseph B. Wirthlin
Finding Peace in Troubled Waters, Art E. Berg
First Nephi: The Doctrinal Foundation, Monte S. Nyman and Charles
     D. Tate, Jr., eds.
Following Christ, Stephen E. Robinson
For the Power Is in Them, Neal A. Maxwell
Foundations for a Happier Marriage, A. Lynn Scoresby
Fourth Nephi through Moroni: From Zion to Destruction, Monte S.
     Nyman and Charles D. Tate, Jr., eds.
Fragments of Experience
From Apostasy to Restoration, Kent P. Jackson
From Prophet to Son, Joseph F. Smith
Gateway We Call Death, Russell M. Nelson

Gems for the Young Folks
Glory of God and Man's Relation to Deity, Hyrum L. Andrus
Glory of God Is Intelligence, Jacob Neusner
Go Forward with Faith: The Biography of Gordon B. Hinckley,
    Sheri L. Dew
God and Man in Eternal Union, Hyrum L. Andrus
God, Man, and the Universe, Hyrum L. Andrus
Gospel and Man's Relationship to Deity, B. H. Roberts
Gospel Doctrine, Joseph F. Smith
Gospel Ideals, David O. McKay
Gospel Kingdom, John Taylor
Gospel Standards, Heber J. Grant
Gospel through the Ages, Milton R. Hunter
Gospel Truth (2 vols.), George Q. Cannon
Government of God, John Taylor
Great Apostasy, James E. Talmage
Great Prologue, Mark E. Petersen
Great Stories from Mormon History, Dean Hughes and Tom Hughes
Greatest Gift, James E. Faust
Growing Up in Zion, Susan Arrington Madsen
Harold B. Lee: Man of Vision, Prophet of God, Francis M. Gibbons
Heavens Are Open, Byron R. Merrill et al., comps.
Heavens Resound, Milton V. Backman, Jr.
Heber J. Grant: Highlights in the Life of a Great Leader, Bryant S.
    Hinckley
Helaman through 3 Nephi 8: According to Thy Word, Monte S.
    Nyman and Charles D. Tate, Jr., eds.
Helping Your Children Stay Morally Clean, Allan K. Burgess
Helps for Missionaries, Hyrum L. Andrus
Henry Ballard, Douglas O. Crookston, ed.
Here We Stand, Joseph Fielding McConkie
Heritage of Faith, Mary E. Stovall and Carol Cornwall Madsen, eds.
High Fives and High Hopes: Favorite Talks Especially for Youth
Higher Laws, Orrin G. Hatch
Highlights in the Life of President David O. McKay, Jeanette McKay
    Morrell
History of Joseph Smith by His Mother, Lucy Mack Smith
History of The Church of Jesus Christ of Latter-day Saints (7 vols.),
    Joseph Smith
Holiness of Everyday Life, Joan B. MacDonald

Home Memories of President David O. McKay, Llewelyn R. McKay, ed.

Home Teaching with Purpose and Power, Richard J. Marshall

Home with Honor, Randy L. Bott

Hope, various General Authorities

House of Glory, S. Michael Wilcox

House of the Lord, James E. Talmage

How to Succeed with People, Stephen R. Covey

How We Got the Bible, Lenet Hadley Read

Howard W. Hunter, Eleanor Knowles

However Long and Hard the Road, Jeffrey R. Holland

Hyrum Smith, Patriarch, Pearson H. Corbett

I Didn't Place in the Talent Race, But . . ., Anya Bateman

I Know That My Redeemer Lives, various General Authorities

I Walk by Faith, Ardeth Greene Kapp

I Walked to Zion, Susan Arrington Madsen

If the Gospel Is True, Why Do I Hurt So Much? Carroll Hofeling Morris

I'm a Day Late and a Dollar Short . . . and It's Okay! Jo Ann Larsen

In Old Nauvoo, George W. Givens

In Search of Truth, John A. Widtsoe

In the Company of Prophets, Heidi S. Swinton

In the Footsteps of Lehi, Warren P. Aston and Michaela Knoth Aston

In the Gospel Net, John A. Widtsoe

In the Lord's Service, Carlos E. Asay

In the Strength of the Lord I Can Do All Things, Carolyn J. Rasmus

In Their Own Words, Carol Cornwall Madsen

Incomparable Christ, Vaughn J. Featherstone

Interesting Account of Several Remarkable Visions, Orson Pratt

Investigating the Book of Mormon Witnesses, Richard Lloyd Anderson

Isaiah and the Prophets, Monte S. Nyman, ed.

Isaiah Plain and Simple, Hoyt W. Brewster, Jr.

Isaiah: Prophet, Seer, and Poet, Victor L. Ludlow

Israel! Do You Know? LeGrand Richards

Italian Mission, Lorenzo Snow

J. Golden Kimball, Claude Richards

Jacob Hamblin, Jacob Hamblin

Jacob through Words of Mormon: To Learn with Joy, Monte S. Nyman and Charles D. Tate, Jr., eds.

Jerusalem: The Eternal City, David B. Galbraith, D. Kelly Ogden, and
Andrew C. Skinner

Jesus Christ, Key to the Plan of Salvation, Gerald N. Lund

Jesus the Christ, James E. Talmage

John Lyon: The Life of a Pioneer Poet, T. Edgar Lyon, Jr.

Joseph Smith and the Doctrine and Covenants, Milton V. Backman,
Jr. and Richard O. Cowan

Joseph Smith and the Law of Consecration, Hyrum L. Andrus

Joseph Smith and the West, Hyrum L. Andrus

Joseph Smith and World Government, Hyrum L. Andrus

Joseph Smith as Scientist, John A. Widtsoe

Joseph Smith Chronology, J. Christopher Conkling

*Joseph Smith Translation: The Restoration of Plain and Precious
Things*, Monte S. Nyman and Robert L. Millet, eds.

Joseph Smith—a Modern Witness for Christ, Hyrum L. Andrus

Joseph Smith, an American Prophet, John Henry Evans

Joseph Smith, the Man and the Seer, Hyrum L. Andrus

Joseph Smith, the Educator, Hyrum L. Andrus

Joseph Smith, the Prophet-Teacher, B. H. Roberts

Joseph Smith: Prophet of the Restoration, Leon R. Hartshorn

Joseph Smith: The Prophet, The Man, Susan Easton Black and
Charles D. Tate, Jr., eds.

Joseph Smith's Commentary on the Bible, Joseph Smith; Kent P.
Jackson, comp. and ed.

Joseph Smith's Idea of the Gospel, Hyrum L. Andrus

Joseph Smith's Kirtland, Karl Ricks Anderson

Joseph Smith's New England Heritage, Richard Lloyd Anderson

Journey to Zion, Carol Cornwall Madsen

Joy of the Journey, Ardeth Greene Kapp

Just for Newlyweds, Brent A. Barlow

Karen's Test, Gladys Clark Farmer

Keepers of the Flame, Janet Peterson and LaRene Gaunt

Keeping Christmas

Key to the Science of Theology, Parley P. Pratt

Knit Together in Love, Carol L. Clark et al.

Labor of Love, Ezra Taft Benson

Latter-day Prophets and the Doctrine and Covenants (4 vols.), Roy
W. Doxey, comp.

Latter-day Prophets and the United States Constitution, Donald Q.
Cannon, ed.

Latter-day Saint Commentary on the Old Testament, Ellis T. Rasmussen

LaVell: Airing It Out, LaVell Edwards with Lee Benson

Learning for the Eternities, Marion G. Romney

Leaves from My Journal, Wilford Woodruff

Lectures on Faith

Lectures on Faith in Historical Perspective, Larry E. Dahl and Charles D. Tate, Jr., eds.

Legacies of Jesus, Lowell L. Bennion

Lehi in the Desert/The World of the Jaredites/There Were Jaredites, Hugh Nibley

Letters Exhibiting the Most Prominent Doctrines of The Church of Jesus Christ of Latter-day Saints, Orson Spencer

Letters of Brigham Young to His Sons, Brigham Young; Dean C. Jessee, ed.

Liberalism, Conservatism, Mormonism, Hyrum L. Andrus

Life of David W. Patten, the First Apostolic Martyr, Lycurgus A. Wilson

Life of Heber C. Kimball, Orson F. Whitney

Life of John Taylor, B. H. Roberts

Life of Joseph F. Smith, Joseph Fielding Smith

Life of Joseph Fielding Smith, Joseph Fielding Smith, Jr., and John J. Stewart

Life of Joseph Smith the Prophet, George Q. Cannon

Life of Joseph the Prophet, Edward W. Tullidge

Life Story of Brigham Young, Susa Young Gates and Leah D. Widtsoe

Light unto the World, David B. Haight

Lighten Up! Chieko N. Okazaki

Lion of the Lord, Susan Easton Black and Larry C. Porter, eds.

Literature of Belief, Neal A. Lambert, ed.

Little Known Friends of the Prophet Joseph Smith, Hyrum L. Andrus

Living by the Power of Faith, Gene R. Cook

Living with Enthusiasm, L. Tom Perry

Look Back at Sodom, Neal A. Maxwell

Lord Needed a Prophet, Susan Arrington Madsen

Lord of the Gospels, Bruce A. Van Orden and Brent L. Top, eds.

Lord's Way, Dallin H. Oaks

Love Is a Verb, Mary Ellen Edmunds

Making Your Home a Missionary Training Center, Joe J. and Barbara K. Christensen

Man May Know for Himself, David O. McKay

Man, His Origin and Destiny, Joseph Fielding Smith
Manuscript Found: The Complete Original "Spaulding Manuscript,"
    Solomon Spaulding
Manuscript History of Brigham Young, Brigham Young
Marathon of Faith, Rex and Janet Lee, with Jim Bell
Marking the Scriptures, Daniel H. Ludlow
Marriage and Divorce, Spencer W. Kimball
Marriage of Equals, Dennis L. Lythgoe
Marriage Talk, Ron Woods
Marvelous Work and a Wonder, LeGrand Richards
Mary Fielding Smith, Daughter of Britain, Don Cecil Corbett
Matthew Cowley Speaks, Matthew Cowley
May Peace Be with You
Meaning of Truth, Alvin R. Dyer
Measure of Our Hearts, Marvin J. Ashton
Mediation and Atonement, John Taylor
Mediator, Boyd K. Packer
Meek and Lowly, Neal A. Maxwell
Men with a Mission, 1837–1841, James B. Allen, Ronald K. Esplin,
    and David J. Whittaker
Message of the Joseph Smith Papyri, Hugh Nibley
Messages for a Happier Life, William B. Smart
Millennial Messiah, Bruce R. McConkie
Missionary Experiences, Preston Nibley
Missouri Persecutions, B. H. Roberts
Moment's Pause
More Excellent Way, Neal A. Maxwell
More Purity Give Me, Vaughn J. Featherstone
Mormon Battalion, B. H. Roberts
Mormon Doctrine of Deity, B. H. Roberts
Mormon Redress Petitions, Clark V. Johnson, ed.
Mormonism and Early Christianity, Hugh Nibley
Mormons and Muslims, Spencer J. Palmer, ed.
Mormonism and the Rise of Western Civilization, Hyrum L. Andrus
Morning Breaks, Howard L. Biddulph
Mortal Messiah (4 vols.), Bruce R. McConkie
Mosiah: Salvation Only through Christ, Monte S. Nyman and
    Charles D. Tate, Jr., eds.
Mothers of the Prophets, Leonard J. Arrington and Susan Arrington
    Madsen
Mount and the Master, Robert E. Wells

My Beloved Sisters, Spencer W. Kimball
My First Mission, George Q. Cannon
My Life's Review, Benjamin F. Johnson
My Neighbor, My Sister, My Friend, Ardeth Greene Kapp
My Parents Married on a Dare and Other Favorite Essays on Life,
    Carlfred Broderick
Needles in the Basket, Beppie Harrison
New Witness for Christ in America (2 vols.), Francis W. Kirkham
New Witness for the Articles of Faith, Bruce R. McConkie
New Witnesses for God (3 vols.), B. H. Roberts
Nibley on the Timely and the Timeless, Hugh Nibley
Notwithstanding My Weakness, Neal A. Maxwell
Nurturing Faith through the Book of Mormon
Of All Things! Hugh Nibley
Of One Heart, Neal A. Maxwell
Old Testament and Related Studies, Hugh Nibley
On Earth As It Is in Heaven, Jeffrey R. Holland and Patricia T.
    Holland
On the Way to Immortality and Eternal Life, J. Reuben Clark
One Flesh, One Heart, Carlfred Broderick
One Step at a Time, Joe J. Christensen
Opening the Seven Seals, Richard D. Draper
Origin of the "Reorganized" Church and the Question of Succession,
    Joseph Fielding Smith
Orson Pratt's Works, Orson Pratt
Our Father's Plan, Boyd K. Packer
Our Latter-day Hymns, Karen Lynn Davidson
Our Search for Happiness, M. Russell Ballard
Our Sisters in the Bible, Jerrie W. Hurd
Our Sisters in the Latter-day Scriptures, Jerrie W. Hurd
Outlines of Ecclesiastical History, B. H. Roberts
Outstanding Stories by General Authorities (3 vols.), Leon R.
    Hartshorn, comp.
Overcoming Depression, Richard King Mower
Overcoming Personal Loss, Duane E. Hiatt
Parent and Teen, Ronald John Zirker
Pearl of Great Price: A History and Commentary, H. Donl Peterson
Pearl of Great Price: Revelations from God, H. Donl Peterson and
    Charles D. Tate, Jr., eds.
Perfect Brightness of Hope, Anita R. Canfield
Personal Writings of Joseph Smith, Joseph Smith; Dean C. Jessee, ed.

Peter and the Popes, A. Burt Horsley
Pioneer Spirit, Heidi S. Swinton
Pioneer Stories, Preston Nibley, comp.
Plain and Precious Things, Neal A. Maxwell
Power of the Word, Robert L. Millet
Power within Us, Russell M. Nelson
Powerful Stories from the Lives of Latter-day Saint Men, Leon R.
    Hartshorn, comp.
Prayer, various General Authorities
Prepare with Honor, Randy L. Bott
Preparing for Christ's Millennial Government, Hyrum L. Andrus
President Kimball Speaks Out, Spencer W. Kimball
Presidents of the Church, Preston Nibley
Priesthood and Church Government, John A. Widtsoe
Principles and Practices of the Restored Gospel, Victor L. Ludlow
Principles of Perfection, Hyrum L. Andrus
Principles, Promises, and Powers, Sterling W. Sill
Prisoner for Conscience' Sake, Bruce A. Van Orden
Program of The Church of Jesus Christ of Latter-day Saints, John A.
    Widtsoe
Progress of Man, Joseph Fielding Smith
Promised Messiah, Bruce R. McConkie
Prophecies and Prophetic Promises from the Doctrine and Covenants,
    Roy W. Doxey
Prophet of the Jubilee, Ronald D. Dennis, trans. and ed.
Prophet Joseph, Larry C. Porter and Susan Easton Black, eds.
Prophetic Book of Mormon, Hugh Nibley
Prophets, Priesthood Keys, and Succession, Hoyt W. Brewster, Jr.
Protecting Your Family in an X-Rated World, Randal A. Wright
Raising Up a Family to the Lord, Gene R. Cook
Rasha the Jew, B. H. Roberts
Rational Theology, John A. Widtsoe
Rays of Living Light, Charles W. Penrose
Reach Up for the Light, James E. Faust
Receiving Answers to Our Prayers, Gene R. Cook
Rediscovering the Book of Mormon, John L. Sorenson and Melvin J.
    Thorne, eds.
Reexploring the Book of Mormon, John W. Welch, ed.
Reflections on Mormonism: Judaeo-Christian Parallels, Truman G.
    Madsen, ed.
Rejoice! His Promises Are Sure, Ardeth Greene Kapp

Relationship of "Mormonism" and Freemasonry, Anthony W. Ivins
Religion and Family Connection, Darwin L. Thomas, ed.
Remarkable Stories from the Lives of Latter-day Saint Women
    (2 vols.), Leon R. Hartshorn, comp.
Renewal of the Earth to Paradisiacal Glory, Hyrum L. Andrus
Repentance, various General Authorities
Restoration of All Things, Joseph Fielding Smith
Restored Church, William E. Berrett
Restored Church of Jesus Christ: the Gospel, Hyrum L. Andrus
Revelations of the Prophet Joseph Smith: A Historical and
    Biographical Commentary of the Doctrine and Covenants,
    Lyndon W. Cook
Rise and Fall of Nauvoo, B. H. Roberts
Sacred Truths of the Doctrine and Covenants (2 vols.), L. G. Otten
    and C. M. Caldwell
Sanctuary, Chieko N. Okazaki
Saturday Night Thoughts, Orson F. Whitney
Saviors on Mount Zion, Archibald F. Bennett
Scientific Aspects of Mormonism, Nels L. Nelson
Scriptures for the Modern World, Paul R. Cheesman and C. Wilfred
    Griggs, eds.
Second American Revolution: Era of Preparation, Hyrum L. Andrus
Second Nephi: The Doctrinal Structure, Monte S. Nyman and Charles
    D. Tate, Jr., eds.
Seek Ye Earnestly, Joseph Fielding Smith
Seek Ye First the Kingdom of God, N. Eldon Tanner
Seeking the Spirit, Joseph Fielding McConkie
Sermon at the Temple and the Sermon on the Mount, John W. Welch
Sermons and Missionary Services of Melvin J. Ballard, Bryant S.
    Hinckley
Serve with Honor, Randy L. Bott
Serving with Strength throughout the World
Seven Claims of the Book of Mormon, John A. Widtsoe and
    Franklin S. Harris, Jr.
Seventy's Course in Theology (5 vols.), B. H. Roberts
Shadowfall, A. Gail Smith
Sharing the Gospel with Others, George Albert Smith
Significance of Gethsemane, Hyrum L. Andrus
Signs of the Times, Joseph Fielding Smith
Simeon Solution, Anne Osborn Poelman
Since Cumorah, Hugh Nibley

Smallest Part, Neal A. Maxwell
So Shall Ye Reap, Ezra Taft Benson
Source of the Light, Maurine Jensen Proctor and Scot Facer Proctor
Spencer W. Kimball: Resolute Disciple, Prophet of God, Francis M.
    Gibbons
Spiritual Plateaus, Glenn L. Pace
Spiritual Progression in the Last Days, Blaine M. Yorgason
Spiritual Roots of Human Relations, Stephen R. Covey
Spiritual Survival in the Last Days, Blaine and Brenton Yorgason
Spirituality and Self-Esteem, Richard L. Bednar and Scott R.
    Peterson
Stalwarts of Mormonism, Preston Nibley
Stand Ye in Holy Places, Harold B. Lee
Steadfast and Immovable, Robert L. Millet
Story and Philosophy of "Mormonism," James E. Talmage
Story of the Book of Abraham, H. Donl Peterson
Story of the Latter-day Saints, James B. Allen and Glen M. Leonard
String of Pearls
Studies in Scripture, Vol. 1: The Doctrine and Covenants, Robert L.
    Millet and Kent P. Jackson, eds.
Studies in Scripture, Vol. 2: The Pearl of Great Price, Robert L. Millet
    and Kent P. Jackson, eds.
Studies in Scripture, Vol. 3: Genesis to 2 Samuel, Kent P. Jackson and
    Robert L. Millet, eds.
Studies in Scripture, Vol. 4: 1 Kings to Malachi, Kent P. Jackson, ed.
Studies in Scripture, Vol. 5: The Gospels, Kent P. Jackson and
    Robert L. Millet, eds.
Studies in Scripture, Vol. 6: Acts to Revelation, Robert L. Millet, ed.
Studies in Scripture, Vol. 7: 1 Nephi to Alma 29, Kent P. Jackson, ed.
Studies in Scripture, Vol. 8: Alma 30 to Moroni, Kent P. Jackson, ed.
Suicide: Some Things We Know, and Some We Do Not, M. Russell
    Ballard
Supporting Saints, Donald Q. Cannon and David J. Whittaker, eds.
Take Heed to Yourselves, Joseph Fielding Smith
Teach Ye Diligently, Boyd K. Packer
Teaching Children Charity, Linda and Richard Eyre
Teaching Children Joy, Linda and Richard Eyre
Teaching Children Responsibility, Linda and Richard Eyre
Teachings of Gordon B. Hinckley, Gordon B. Hinckley
Teachings of the Doctrine and Covenants, William E. Berrett

Teachings of the Prophet Joseph Smith, Joseph Smith; comp. Joseph Fielding Smith

Teens, Temple Marriage, and Eternity, Allan K. Burgess

Temple and Cosmos, Hugh Nibley

Temple in Antiquity, Truman G. Madsen, ed.

Temples of the Ancient World, Donald W. Parry, ed.

Ten Commandments Today

That My Family Should Partake, Neal A. Maxwell

That We Might Have Joy, Howard W. Hunter

They Knew the Prophet, Hyrum L. Andrus and Helen Mae Andrus, comps.

Things As They Really Are, Neal A. Maxwell

Things I Wish I'd Known Sooner, Jaroldeen Edwards

Third Nephi 9–30: This Is My Gospel, Monte S. Nyman and Charles D. Tate, Jr., eds.

This Nation Shall Endure, Ezra Taft Benson

Thoughts of a Grasshopper, Louise Plummer

Thriving on Our Differences, Karen Lynn Davidson

Thy People Shall Be My People and Thy God My God

Time to Choose, Neal A. Maxwell

Tinkling Cymbals and Sounding Brass, Hugh Nibley

To Draw Closer to God, Henry B. Eyring

To Reach Even unto You, James E. Faust

To Rejoice As Women, Susette Fletcher Green and Dawn Hall Anderson, eds.

To Strengthen Their Faith in Christ, Hyrum L. Andrus

True Design and Order of World Government, Hyrum L. Andrus

Twelve Traps in Today's Marriage and How to Avoid Them, Brent A. Barlow

Understandable Religion, John A. Widtsoe

Understanding Death, Brent A. Barlow, ed.

Understanding Paul, Richard Lloyd Anderson

Unique Melody, Norma B. Ashton

Unknown Testament, Lowell L. Bennion

Unlocking the Old Testament, Victor L. Ludlow

View of the Hebrews: 1825 2nd Edition Complete Text, Ethan Smith; Charles D. Tate, Jr., ed.

Visions of Zion, Alexander B. Morrison

Visiting Teaching, Johanna Flynn and Anita Canfield

Vitality of Mormonism, James E. Talmage

Voice of Israel's Prophets, Sidney B. Sperry

Voice of Warning, Parley P. Pratt
Walk Tall, You're a Daughter of God, Jamie Glenn
War and Saints, Hyrum L. Andrus
Warfare in the Book of Mormon, Stephen D. Ricks and William J. Hamblin, eds.
Watch and Be Ready
Way to Perfection, Joseph Fielding Smith
We Talk of Christ, We Rejoice in Christ, Neal A. Maxwell
We Will Prove Them Herewith, Neal A. Maxwell
We'll Bring the World His Truth, Dean Hughes and Tom Hughes
Welsh Mormon Writings from 1844 to 1862, Ronald D. Dennis
What Happy Families Are Doing, Eric G. Stephan and Judith Stephan Smith
What Husbands Expect of Wives, Brent A. Barlow
What I Wish I'd Known in High School (2 vols.), John Bytheway
What Latter-day Stripling Warriors Learn from Their Mothers, Ardeth Greene Kapp
What Wives Expect of Husbands, Brent A. Barlow
When a Child Wanders, Robert L. Millet
When a Loved One Dies, Kathleen Rawlings Buntin, with Shawn Dennis Buntin, Terri Kathleen Buntin, Shane Darrell Buntin
When Drugs Hit Home, Lewis B. Hancock
Where Is Wisdom? Stephen L Richards
Where Jesus Walked, D. Kelly Ogden
Wherefore, Ye Must Press Forward, Neal A. Maxwell
Who Am I? Alvin R. Dyer
Why Does My Mother's Day Potted Plant Always Die? Janene Wolsey Baadsgaard
Why Say No When the World Says Yes? Randal A. Wright, comp.
Why Stay Morally Clean, Boyd K. Packer
Why the King James Version, J. Reuben Clark, Jr.
Wilford Woodruff, His Life and Labors, Matthias F. Cowley
Will a Man Rob God? Milton R. Hunter
William Clayton's Journal, William Clayton
Willpower Is Not Enough, A. Dean Byrd and Mark D. Chamberlain
Within Reach, Robert L. Millet
With Knowledge and Spiritual Power, Hyrum L. Andrus
Witness and a Warning, Ezra Taft Benson
Witness of Jesus Christ, Richard D. Draper, ed.
Witness of the Light, Scot Facer Proctor
Woman, various General Authorities

Woman and the Priesthood, Rodney Turner
Woman to Woman
Woman's Reach, Belle S. Spafford
Women and Christ, Dawn Hall Anderson, Susette Fletcher Green,
    and Marie Cornwall, eds.
Women and the Power Within, Dawn Hall Anderson and Marie
    Cornwall, eds.
Women in the Covenant of Grace, Dawn Hall Anderson and Susette
    Fletcher Green, eds.
Women of Covenant, Jill Mulvay Derr, Janath Russell Cannon, and
    Maureen Ursenbach Beecher
Women of Mormondom (Excerpts), Edward W. Tullidge
Women of Wisdom and Knowledge, Marie Cornwall and Susan
    Howe, eds.
Women Steadfast in Christ, Dawn Hall Anderson and Marie
    Cornwall, eds.
Women's Voices, Kenneth W. Godfrey, Audrey M. Godfrey, and Jill
    Mulvay Derr, eds.
Wondrous Power of a Mother, Gordon B. Hinckley and Marjorie P.
    Hinckley
Word of Wisdom: a Modern Interpretation, John A. Widtsoe and
    Leah D. Widtsoe
Words of Joseph Smith, Joseph Smith; Andrew F. Ehat and
    Lyndon W. Cook, eds.
Words of the Twelve Prophets, Monte S. Nyman, Farres H. Nyman
World and the Prophets, Hugh Nibley
Worth Waiting For, Brent A. Barlow
Writings of Camilla Eyring Kimball, Camilla Eyring Kimball
You Can Learn to Speak, Royal L. Garff
You, Your Family, and the Scriptures, Ed J. Pinegar
Young Lions, Barbara A. Lewis
Youth Leading Youth, Shane R. Barker

APOCRYPHA AND PSEUDEPIGRAPHA

NOTE: The Apocrypha and Pseudepigrapha are available in the
Books window when using Disk B. (Click the Non-LDS Authors
button.) They are arranged in three collections: Old Testament
Apocrypha, Old Testament Pseudepigrapha, and New Testament
Pseudepigrapha.

Acts and Martyrdom of St. Matthew the Apostle
Acts and Martyrdom of the Holy Apostle Andrew
Acts of Andrew and Matthias
Acts of Barnabas
Acts of Paul and Thecla
Acts of Peter and Andrew
Acts of Philip
Acts of the Holy Apostle and Evangelist John the Theologian
Acts of the Holy Apostle Thaddaeus
Acts of the Holy Apostle Thomas
Acts of the Holy Apostles Peter and Paul
Apocalypse of Adam
Apocalypse of Moses
Apostolic Canons
Avenging of the Saviour
Baruch
Book of Enoch (Ethiopic)
Book of John Concerning the Falling Asleep of Mary
Consummation of Thomas the Apostle
Daniel and Susanna
Daniel, Bel, and the Snake
Death of Pilate
Ecclesiasticus or the Wisdom of Jesus Son of Sirach
First Book of Adam and Eve
First Book of Esdras
First Book of the Maccabees
Giving Up of Pontius Pilate
Gospel of Nicodemus (Acta Pilati)
Gospel of Peter
Gospel of Pseudo-Matthew
Gospel of the Nativity of Mary
Gospel of Thomas
History of Joseph the Carpenter
Judith
Letter of Jeremiah
Letter of Pontius Pilate
Martyrdom of the Holy and Glorious Apostle Bartholomew
Narrative of Joseph
Passing of Mary
Prayer of Azariah
Prayer of Manasseh

Protoevangelium of James
Report of Pontius Pilate
Rest of the Chapters of the Book of Esther
Revelation of Esdras
Revelation of John
Revelation of Moses
Revelation of Paul
Revelation of Peter
Second Book of Esdras
Second Book of the Maccabees
Slavonic Vita Adae et Evae (Life of Adam and Eve from the Slavonic)
Song of the Three
Testament of Abraham
Testaments of the Twelve Patriarchs
Tobit
Vision of Paul
Vita Adae et Evae (Life of Adam and Eve)
Wisdom of Solomon

EARLY CHRISTIAN WRITINGS

NOTE: The Early Christian Writings are available in the Books window when using Disk B. (Click the Non-LDS Authors button.)

Ad Scapula, Tertullian
Address to the Greeks, Tatian
Against All Heresies, Tertullian
Against Apion, Flavius Josephus
Against Heresies, Irenaeus of Lyons
Against the Pelagians, Jerome
Apologies for the Christians, Justin Martyr
Apology, Tertullian
Barlaam and Ioasaph, John Damascene
Catechetical Lectures, Cyril
City of God, Augustine
Commentary on John, Origen
Commentary on Matthew, Origen
Confessions, Augustine
Contra Celsum, Origen
De Fuga in Persecutione, Tertullian
De Principiis, Origen

De Spiritu Sancto, Basil the Great
De Synodis, Athanasius
Dialogue with Trypho, Justin Martyr
Didache
Divine Institutes, Lactantius
Ecclesiastical History, Eusebius of Caesarea
Ecclesiastical History, Socrates Scholasticus
Ecclesiastical History, Sozomen
Epistle of Barnabas, Barnabas
Epistle to Diognetus, Mathetes
Epistle to the Philippians, Polycarp
Epistles of Clement of Rome, Clement of Rome
Epistles of Cyprian, Cyprian
Epistles of Ignatius, Ignatius
Extant Fragments, Dionysus
Five Books against Marcion, Tertullian
Fragment of the Lost Work on the Resurrection, Justin Martyr
Fragments from the Acts of the Church, Hegesippus
Fragments, Irenaeus of Lyons
Fragments, Papias
Gospel According to Peter, Pseudo-Peter
Homilies on Acts, John Chrysostom
Homilies on the Epistle to the Hebrews, John Chrysostom
Homilies on the Epistle to the Romans, John Chrysostom
Homilies on the Gospel According to Matthew, John Chrysostom
Homilies on the Gospel of John, John Chrysostom
Hortatory Address to the Greeks, Justin Martyr
Life of Constantine, Eusebius of Caesarea
Martyrdom of Polycarp
Martyrdom of the Holy Martyrs
Narrative of Zosimus
Octavius, Minucius Felix
On Christian Doctrine, Augustine
On Modesty, Tertullian
On Monogamy, Tertullian
On the Councils, Hilary
On the Incarnation of the Word, Athanasius
On the Resurrection, Tertullian
On the Trinity, Augustine
Paedagogus, Clement of Alexandria
Pastor, Hermas

Proslogion (Excerpts), Anselm
Recognitions, Clement of Rome
Revelation of Peter, Pseudo-Peter
Scorpiace, Tertullian
Selected Letters of Ambrose, Ambrose
Selected Letters of Basil the Great, Basil the Great
Stromata, Clement of Alexandria
Treatise on the Priesthood, John Chrysostom
Treatises, Cyprian

WORLD CLASSICS LIBRARY

NOTE: The World Classics Library is available in the Books window when using Disk B. (Click the Non-LDS Authors button.)

 RELIGION

Analects, Confucius
Antiquities of the Jews, Flavius Josephus
Foxe's Book of Martyrs, John Foxe
Grace Abounding on the Chief of Sinners, John Bunyan
Heretics, G. K. Chesterton
Institutes of the Christian Religion, John Calvin
Large Catechism, Martin Luther
Life and Times of Jesus the Messiah, Alfred Edersheim (5 vols.)
Life of Christ, Frederic Farrar
Little Flowers, Francis of Assisi
Ninety-Five Theses, Martin Luther
Old Testament Bible History, Alfred Edersheim (7 vols.)
Orthodoxy, G. K. Chesterton
Plain Account of Christian Perfection, John Wesley
Smalcald Articles, Martin Luther
Summa Theologica, Thomas Aquinas (5 vols.)
Temple at the Time of Christ, Alfred Edersheim
Thesis on the King James Version, Edgar A. Goodspeed
Translators to the Reader (of the King James Version of the Bible)
Treatise on Good Works, Martin Luther

 PHILOSOPHY

Apology, Plato
Athenian Constitution, Aristotle

Code of Hammurabi, Hammurabi
Consolation of Philosophy, Boethius
Critique of Pure Reason, Immanuel Kant
Crito, Plato
Discourse on Reason, René Descartes
Essay Concerning Human Understanding, John Locke
Essays of Michel de Montaigne, Michel de Montaigne
Essays of Ralph Waldo Emerson, Ralph Waldo Emerson
Essays of Sir Francis Bacon, Francis Bacon
Inequality of Man, Jean Jacques Rousseau
In Praise of Folly, Desiderius Erasmus
Letter Concerning Toleration, John Locke
Leviathan, Thomas Hobbes
Meditations, Marcus Aurelius
Metaphysics of Morals, Immanuel Kant
Metaphysics, Aristotle
Moral Discourses, Epictetus
Nicomachean Ethics, Aristotle
On Civil Government, John Locke
On the Improvement of the Understanding, Baruch Spinoza
On the Soul, Aristotle
Pensées, Blaise Pascal
Phaedo, Plato
Physics, Aristotle
Poetics, Aristotle
Politics, Aristotle
Prince, Nicolo Machiavelli
Republic, Plato
Social Contract (Excerpts), Jean Jacques Rousseau
Sophist, Plato
Symposium, Plato
Timaeus, Plato
Utilitarianism, John Stuart Mill
Utopia, Thomas More
Varieties of Religious Experience, William James
Walden, Henry David Thoreau
Wealth of Nations, Adam Smith
Will to Believe, William James

INSPIRATION

Acres of Diamonds, Russell Conwell
As a Man Thinketh, James Allen
Imitation of Christ, Thomas à Kempis
In His Steps, Charles Sheldon
Lives of the Noble Grecians and Romans, Plutarch
Men of Invention and Industry, Samuel Smiles

 BIOGRAPHY

Abraham Lincoln, James Russell Lowell
Autobiography of Benjamin Franklin, Benjamin Franklin
Father Damien, Robert Louis Stevenson
Life of Flavius Josephus, Flavius Josephus
Narrative of the Life of Frederick Douglass, Frederick Douglass
Thomas Jefferson, Edward Ellis

 AMERICAN HISTORY

Account of the British Surrender, Ebenezer Denny
Account of the Ordeal at Valley Forge, Waldo Albigence
American Notes, Charles Dickens
Articles of Confederation
Common Sense, Thomas Paine
Constitution of the United States of America
Declaration of Independence
Declaration of the First Continental Congress
Declaration of the Rights of Man and of the Citizen
Declaration of the Second Continental Congress
Democracy in America, Alexis de Tocqueville
Emancipation Proclamation, Abraham Lincoln
Farewell Address, George Washington
Federalist Papers
First Inaugural Address, Abraham Lincoln
Gettysburg Address, Abraham Lincoln
Give Me Liberty or Give Me Death, Patrick Henry
Inaugural Address, John Adams
Inaugural Address, Thomas Jefferson
Letter Presenting the Constitution
Letter to the King and Queen of Spain, Christopher Columbus
Mayflower Compact
Midnight Ride of Paul Revere, Henry Wadsworth Longfellow

Monroe Doctrine
Paris Peace Treaty of 1783
Plan for Union, William Penn
Remarks to Congress, Henry Clay
Resolutions of the Stamp Act Congress
Rights of Man, Thomas Paine
Rights of the Colonists, Samuel Adams
Second Inaugural Address, Abraham Lincoln
Speech on the Stamp Act, William Pitt
Steep Trails, John Muir
Subsequent Amendments to the Constitution
United States Bill of Rights

 WORLD HISTORY

Anglo-Saxon Chronicle
Annals, Tacitus
Commentaries on the Gallic and Civil Wars, Julius Caesar
Crossing, Winston Churchill
Decline and Fall of the Roman Empire, Edward Gibbon
Fall of Troy, Smyrnaeus
Histories, Tacitus
History, Herodotus
History of the Peloponnesian War, Thucydides
Magna Charta
Sketches of Jewish Social Life, Alfred Edersheim
Uncommercial Traveller, Charles Dickens
Wars of the Jews, Flavius Josephus

 MYTHOLOGY

Aeneid, Virgil
Aesop's Fables, Aesop
Beowulf
Chronicle of the Cid, Robert Southey
Four Arthurian Romances, Chrétien de Troyes
Iliad, Homer
Indian Why Stories, Frank Linderman
Metamorphoses, Ovid
Mythology, Thomas Bullfinch
Myths and Legends of the Sioux, Marie McLaughlin

Odyssey, Homer
Theogony, Hesiod

 FICTION

Adventures of Huckleberry Finn, Mark Twain
Adventures of Tom Sawyer, Mark Twain
Anna Karenina, Leo Tolstoy
Anne of Avonlea, Lucy M. Montgomery
Anne of Green Gables, Lucy M. Montgomery
Around the World in Eighty Days, Jules Verne
At the Back of the North Wind, George Macdonald
Billy Budd, Herman Melville
Brothers Karamazov, Fyodor Dostoevsky
Christmas Carol, Charles Dickens
Connecticut Yankee in King Arthur's Court, Mark Twain
Crime and Punishment, Fyodor Dostoevsky
David Copperfield, Charles Dickens
Death of Ivan Ilych, Leo Tolstoy
Don Quixote, Miguel Cervantes
Emma, Jane Austen
Excerpts from the Diary of Adam, Mark Twain
Gift of the Magi, O. Henry
Great Expectations, Charles Dickens
Great Stone Face, Nathaniel Hawthorne
Gulliver's Travels, Jonathan Swift
Hard Times, Charles Dickens
House of the Seven Gables, Nathaniel Hawthorne
Jane Eyre, Charlotte Brontë
Journey to the Center of the Earth, Jules Verne
Jungle Book, Rudyard Kipling
Just So Stories, Rudyard Kipling
Kidnapped, Robert Louis Stevenson
Last of the Mohicans, James Fenimore Cooper
Les Misérables, Victor Hugo
Lilith, George Macdonald
Little Lord Fauntleroy, Francis H. Burnett
Little Women, Louisa May Alcott
Lost Prince, Francis H. Burnett
Man in the Iron Mask, Alexandre Dumas
Mansfield Park, Jane Austen

Mansion, Henry Van Dyke
Master and Man, Leo Tolstoy
Merry Adventures of Robin Hood, Howard Pyle
Moby Dick, Herman Melville
Nicholas Nickleby, Charles Dickens
Notes from the Underground, Fyodor Dostoevsky
O Pioneers! Willa Cather
Old Curiosity Shop, Charles Dickens
Oliver Twist, Charles Dickens
Persuasion, Jane Austen
Phantastes, George Macdonald
Pickwick Papers, Charles Dickens
Picture of Dorian Gray, Oscar Wilde
Pilgrim's Progress, John Bunyan
Pride and Prejudice, Jane Austen
Prince and the Pauper, Mark Twain
Princess and Curdie, George Macdonald
Princess and the Goblin, George Macdonald
Red Badge of Courage, Stephen Crane
Robinson Crusoe, Daniel Defoe
Scarlet Letter, Nathaniel Hawthorne
Secret Garden, Francis H. Burnett
Sense and Sensibility, Jane Austen
Silas Marner, George Eliot
Swiss Family Robinson, Johann David Wyss
Tale of Two Cities, Charles Dickens
Treasure Island, Robert Louis Stevenson
Twenty Thousand Leagues under the Sea, Jules Verne
Uncle Tom's Cabin, Harriet Beecher Stowe
War and Peace, Leo Tolstoy
White Fang, Jack London
Wisdom of Father Brown, G. K. Chesterton
Wuthering Heights, Emily Brontë

 POETRY

Book of Thel, William Blake
Chambered Nautilus, Oliver Wendell Holmes
Child's Garden of Verses, Robert Louis Stevenson
Divine Comedy, Dante Alighieri (3 vols.)
Essay on Man, Alexander Pope

Heap o' Livin', Edgar A. Guest
Idylls of the King, Alfred, Lord Tennyson
Ivanhoe, Walter Scott
Lyrical Ballads, William Wordsworth
Moral Emblems, Robert Louis Stevenson
Ode on Intimations of Immortality, William Wordsworth
Paradise Lost, John Milton
Paradise Regained, John Milton
Prelude, William Wordsworth
Rime of the Ancient Mariner, Samuel Taylor Coleridge
Selected Poems of Ella Wheeler Wilcox, Ella Wheeler Wilcox
Selected Poems of George Herbert, George Herbert
Selected Poems of John Keats, John Keats
Selected Poems of Joyce Kilmer, Joyce Kilmer
Selected Poems of Rupert Brooke, Rupert Brooke
Song of Hiawatha, Henry Wadsworth Longfellow
Songs of Innocence and of Experience, William Blake
Sonnets, William Shakespeare

 DRAMA

All's Well That Ends Well, William Shakespeare
Antony and Cleopatra, William Shakespeare
As You Like It, William Shakespeare
Comedy of Errors, William Shakespeare
Coriolanus, William Shakespeare
Cymbeline, William Shakespeare
Hamlet, William Shakespeare
Julius Caesar, William Shakespeare
King Henry IV, part 1, William Shakespeare
King Henry IV, part 2, William Shakespeare
King Henry V, William Shakespeare
King Henry VI, part 1, William Shakespeare
King Henry VI, part 2, William Shakespeare
King Henry VI, part 3, William Shakespeare
King Henry VIII, William Shakespeare
King John, William Shakespeare
King Lear, William Shakespeare
King Richard II, William Shakespeare
King Richard III, William Shakespeare
Love's Labours Lost, William Shakespeare

Macbeth, William Shakespeare
Measure for Measure, William Shakespeare
Merchant of Venice, William Shakespeare
Merry Wives of Windsor, William Shakespeare
Midsummer Night's Dream, William Shakespeare
Much Ado about Nothing, William Shakespeare
Oedipus the King, Sophocles
Othello, William Shakespeare
Pericles, Prince of Tyre, William Shakespeare
Prometheus Bound, Euripides
Pygmalion, George Bernard Shaw
Romeo and Juliet, William Shakespeare
Taming of the Shrew, William Shakespeare
Tempest, William Shakespeare
Timon of Athens, William Shakespeare
Titus Andronicus, William Shakespeare
Troilus and Cressida, William Shakespeare
Twelfth Night, William Shakespeare
Two Gentlemen of Verona, William Shakespeare
Winter's Tale, William Shakespeare

INDEX